THE WORD

THE

ISRAELITES

AND THE

DAMNED

Edited by Shadrock

**THIS BOOK IS NOT DIRECTED
AGAINST ANY PHILOSOPHY
BUT RATHER AGAINST
THE PRACTITIONERS
OF THE EVIL LIE**

**THE LIE THAT HAS CAUSED MUCH TURMOIL
AMONG A PEOPLE WHO ONCE KNEW AND
LIVED BY THE TRUTH**

FOR MORE INFORMATION ON
THE CHILDREN OF ISRAEL
WITH BIBLICAL AND HISTORICAL PROOF
YOU MUST READ

THE TRUTH THE LIE AND THE BIBLE
and
THE FORGOTTEN ISRAELITES
Written By Shadrock

Fifth Ribb Publishing
6951 Olive Blvd
University City, MO 63130

ISBN *978-1736789834*

THE WORD THE ISRAELITES AND THE DAMNED

CONTENTS

PREFACE

I will be using this section of the book to tell a little story, and at the same time introduce the other writers.

Prior to the time of the summer of 1985, I was choked with the urge to get out what was inside, and teach my people about this truth, but I would always return home really choked. Choked with emotion, for I thought it very strange, that black people would not listen to a single word I was saying.

I reached a point in my life when I did not know whom I'd given up on, whether I had given up on myself or my people, I just knew I had given up.

Matthew 10:22-23 "And ye shall be hated of all men for my name's sake: but he that endureth to the end shall be saved. But when they persecute you in this city, flee ye into another: for verily I say unto you, **Ye shall not have gone over the cities of Israel, till the Son of man be come.**"

Verse 23 explains that Jesus knew how difficult it would be to teach this truth, for He said that He would go and come again, and Israel would not come to the knowledge of this doctrine to accept it fully. Yet today we hear of the millions and millions that are followers of the pagan philosophy called Christianity. This had been predicted by John in the book of Revelation as the Great Whore. When the multitude came to Jesus the Christ, in His day on earth, they wanted to be healed of their sicknesses, or to try to prove Him wrong by asking questions that were irrelevant and stupid. They never actually followed Him, understanding His doctrine.

I also remembered that Jesus was not speaking to the world then, as Christians would want us to believe, but to His own, the twelve that represented the children of Israel. He also set the stage to show us what the characteristics of the children of Israel would be like in times to come. Out of the twelve, there was a stranger (a Canaanite), one that betrayed Him, and one that denied Him. **Matthew 10:2-4** reveals the make up of my people in these last days.

Friday nights were the worst, because this night was suppose to be the beginning of my Sabbath. I could not stay at home. I would roam the streets seeking worldly pleasures to satisfy a fire that was burning within me. A fire that my little room could not put out, for it was in this little room, where I once lived that I heard the voice telling me to go out and teach this doctrine. At first it was O.K., but after trying and failing every time, it created a burning pain that became unbearable. To put it mildly, my life was a mess. Anyhow, another interest was always there in my storeroom of gifts - my music. So I decided to pursue it. My music story would be a long one, so I'll cut it short.

I met Tony Castrilli in 1983 and employed him as my keyboard player, because I had made up my mind that music is where I would focus. No more God, no more trying to convert black people into the doctrine of truth. Besides, I had discovered that if you really want to get my people mad, tell them the truth. Tell them that their Christian church is not of God. Tell them that it is a white pagan philosophy started in Rome, based on pagan practices and customs. You can say it of course, but you must have a pair of good legs and make sure they don't fail you.

For two years I worked at my music, dreaming of creating my own Motown. I worked hard at it. I recorded my first album. Things were beginning to shape the way I wanted, but the voice would not go away. Then suddenly, Tony got really sick with his allergies. Allergies that usually went away after a time he said. I always had this problem he reminded me, but as time dragged on he was getting worse, and he could not play anymore. So one day in the summer of '85, I visited him to see how he was doing. He looked awful, so then I had decided that I would find another keyboard player, after all I told myself they are a dime a dozen. But during that visit something happened that changed the course of my thinking and eventually the course of my life.

Tony started talking about God to me. Now this is a subject that I had vowed never to be resurrected anymore in any conversation that I might have in the future. He, nevertheless blabbered on, until it got to me, and I told him that everything he said was confusing to me, and that God was black. I must admit, this statement was not said in a way to win his soul. I was downright sarcastic, while he was acting so enthusiastic. I wanted to know why the heck any Italian would want to know about this strange teaching.

I was mad, but Tony was not. He said among other spoken words, and I will never forget what he said. "Shad, if you prove it to me in the bible, I would believe you, for I don't care what God looks like. I want to serve Him." But he did not stop there as most Christians would have done. No, he continued to say that he wanted to know the truth. That day was my first day of teaching this doctrine in a formal, yet in a way informal. It was to an Italian who wanted to know the truth about the God of Israel.

The school was opened and classes were kept every Friday morning at Tony's house when his parents were not there. I would go over with my bible and he would invite other Italians in the neighbourhood. I dared not have kept the school on Saturdays (Sabbath) when his parents were home. This was the beginning of the teaching of this doctrine in Canada.

The first Passover was an experience in itself. While we were praying and breaking bread in one area of his house, everything was falling down in other parts of the house. The phone began to ring, the Big Ben clock began to chime. It was some experience. I guess the other forces were really mad.

With everything that was happening around me, I was still shocked to know that not one black person was interested in this doctrine. Here I was surrounded by Italians and white people, something I was never accustomed to. Yet there was so much love. A love that I often wished was among my own. My thoughts were silent anyhow.

These Italians were now my brethren. They were people who wanted to learn the truth. People who were sincere and receptive of pure knowledge. People whom I have grown to love with all my heart.

This experience got me a little scared. I knew somewhere inside of me that I had to deliver this message before I died. So now you can understand why I was so scared. I thought that my life would be coming to an end, and that was why people were beginning to listen. I even remembered Paul's gift to teach the Gentiles, but that was God's punishment to Paul, but what had I done? My consolation was in the way my brethren accepted the doctrine of Israel, which was suppose to be a black thing. I remembered the respect the Roman soldier paid to the Christ, that allowed Jesus to say that such faith He had not found in all Israel, and here I was having this very same experience in my life. **Matthew 8:8-10**. I remembered the story of Jesus telling His twelve how difficult this message was going to be. Anyhow, through the years many black people came but mostly to criticize, to find fault, and even fight, but me knowing better, did better. In those days there were so many men who called themselves Reverends, Pastors and Preachers, even Muslims and Rastafarians that had passed through the doors, but none understood. Did you ever stop to think why when Jesus was teaching, and speaking to the multitude, He would always say, "those who have ears to hear let them hear, and those who have eyes to see let them see." Well, we all have eyes and ears. Then why did He keep on saying that? **Matthew 11:15**. He knew that everyone could not really understand the doctrine of the Israelites.

We have endured and now we are teaching this doctrine to the world. The following are Israelite writers from the House of Israel here in Canada who are making their mark on God's truth. **Tony Castrilli** is now a teacher in the House of Israel. He had studied and studied. He had asked more questions than most people did at that time. Eventually I told him to go out, read any book, talk to any Christian teacher, or priest and analyze the answers they give, then compare it with what the bible teaches. In other words prove me wrong. He didn't because he couldn't prove me wrong. Tony's article is called **"Through the Eyes of a Roman."** This is a chapter about the truth concerning the Israelites, written by an Italian dedicated to the spreading of this message to all nations.

Lina Vescio is also an Italian with a heart as big as Rome where she was born. She grew up, lived and married in Canada and was once a devout Catholic. She was among the first, and still is one of the hardest workers that ever accepted this truth about the God of Israel. She is a favourite and well loved among the brethren. Her eyes are now opened, and she too is a teacher in the House of Israel. Lina's article is called **"The Heart of a Woman."** It is an account given of courage, the courage to speak out, and to embrace the truth regardless of the consequences.

E.F. Paterson is not a typical Canadian. She was a Christian missionary who settled in Spain for a number of years. With her background, the doctrine of Israel was at first hard to accept, being a white person. All the questions she had as a Christian missionary, that could not have been answered then by her previous teachings, were answered when she came through the gates of The House of Israel. Her article is called **"The Silenced One."** This is a brief, but explainable history of the white Christian male dominance even over his own woman. A history of the sufferings of European women, by the hand of the Christian church.

It took me another four years of teaching before it happened. In 1989 after trying so hard to reach out, the first black face appeared in the likeness of Michael Hinds, and he has been a good soldier for Israel ever since.

Michael Hinds entered our school a quiet and humble person. He never asked questions at first, because silently he too was trying to put the pieces together. Like I've always said, try hard to prove me wrong. Buy books and read, go to the library and study, do whatever you can and if you can't prove me wrong, you will begin to understand. Mike did just that, he too soon became a dedicated student. This doctrine cannot be had from the conventional church or school. You must pray for the spirit of understanding. Mike did discover his hidden gift of that spirit. He is a natural researcher and communicator, and that is why today he is an Investigative Researcher for The House of Israel. Michael's articles are called **"The Philosophical Background of the Israelis"** and **"The Israelites - God's Elect."** In these chapters Michael will be revealing the hidden facts which impact our daily lives.

Garth Bobb is a young man who was prepared for the task ahead by Michael Hinds. Michael introduced the doctrine of Israel to this young man who had a fascinating background of radicalism based on the ideological foundation of black nationalism. Garth is one of many aspiring leaders in the

House of Israel. At this time he is President of R.I.S.E. (Restoring Israelites Self-Awareness through Education), a youth arm of the House of Israel.

"The Ark of the Covenant." A detailed and common sense approach to this subject that is now being kicked around by others who are not qualified to speak on it.

I am so proud, and happy that I was able to make a difference in all of their lives, by guiding them on the path of truth. These soldiers of Israel are now effectively armed, not only to do battle with the enemy of God, but also to teach His word, helping me to carry this burden, which was so very heavy even for the Prophets to bare. I thank them as their teacher, for doing the will of our God, the God of our Fathers, the God of Abraham, the God of Isaac, and the God of Jacob, the Holy One of Israel.

This book acts as a training ground for these new writers who want to say something of importance to this world of philosophical corruption and confusion. This book wants to talk about...

THE ROSE AND THE RAIN

There once was a rose that stood tall and strong
But now lies listless on the ground
What once was glorious in beauty
Is now trodden underfoot
The bees no longer stop to drink of its sweet nectar
But just pass on by as if nothing stands there
The sweetness of its scent
Has drifted away with the wind
No longer a beckoning force
This flower which was so full of purity
Became stripped of its worth and dignity
But time is at hand to replant and grow up strong
The God of Israel has poured His rain
Upon the ground where it stands
The petals are about to bloom
And the roots have taken strong hold
Never again will this flower be overlooked
But will be replenished in the earth
And the world shall witness the rebirth of the Rose.

INTRODUCTION

Dear reader, there are some things that we need to clarify, judging from the questions being asked by some of you after reading my first two books, **"The Truth The Lie And The Bible"** and **"The Forgotten Israelites."**

One of your main concerns deals with whether or not I am a racist, or if the teachings and lessons written in my books are only for black people. The answer is no. I am not a racist, and two; the lessons are not only for black people. You wanted to know how then can others fit into the religion of the Israelites. A few who had contact before with others, who claimed to be Israelites, whose leadership refused to accept any other race other than Afro-Americans within their group, are now worried that I might be teaching other races directly or indirectly.

Now let me have my say. First of all, when we were all sailing in the midst of the philosophical sea, tossed to and fro by the wind of confusion. When there was only the urge to serve God. When we didn't even care what He looked like. When the pain in our bodies grew like the sweat on our backs, and tears were natural to the eye. When death was our only way out of torment, we listened to a philosophy that taught us to love the world, and we were prepared to do just that. Today this same philosophy is so strong within us that now we are not only prepared to kill for it, but to die for it also. Ask yourself a very simple question. What is it that made this philosophy so strong? Your answer to this question will be the answer to your life and your future.

When we were without knowledge of self, without the wisdom to understand that knowledge, without the understanding of purpose, we copied. Some by choice, others by force, but all of us copied to survive. The white Christian male never preached racism to the blackman. He demonstrated it with his actions. He never said this is a white philosophy and that it is only for white people. He demonstrated the fact that when you read the bible the way he taught you, all you ever saw was the white images. When you look at him, and at the images, they all look alike, so naturally you would have to believe that God was white and Jesus was white. Also that all the Prophets were white, hereby admitting that you are no good. You cannot be of God and suffer the way you do. No! You are now saying to yourself and others, look at those white people, they have everything and we have nothing. Look at those white people, they even look like Jesus with their long hair and look at mine, burnt and hard, woolly and tough. Look at those white people, they own all the massive and beautiful looking churches made out of marble, with the most expensive wood, and look at ours, shabby and old. Look at those white people, most of them are so rich they control the world and look at us, we can't even live together in this ghetto. Then you add it all up and come to the conclusion that you are going to do everything the white man is doing, serve the same god he is serving, eat the same food he is eating, but most importantly, that you are going to walk in his footsteps. This is a reality today. When you want to denounce the whiteness in his festive season, you create a black one called "Kwanza."

I remembered being corrected once for making this statement. I was told that "Kwanza" means "harvest of the first fruits." Now can anyone tell me what kind of fruit you will be harvesting at this time of year - in this most evil, cold, and dark time?

From December 21st to 25th is originally a pagan celebration, but it does not stop there. It goes on to the end of the pagan year, then replaced by the celebration of Janus (January), the pagan god. We should have been denouncing the season altogether.

When we get tired of the white Jesus on the cross, some black Christians replace Him with a black one, when we should have been getting rid of the cross. As a matter of fact we should have been getting rid of Christianity, but we have become so wrapped up in skin-colour and the emotional aspect of the Christian church, that we no longer look at anything else. Logic becomes a foreign language.

Sometimes I wonder, why the followers of Jim Jones lined-up to drink poison? The answer to this question is very frightening. Some of us see the danger, yet we tarry on for the sake of tradition, refusing to take instructions from God through His Prophets written in the scriptures, and this is our biggest mistake.

If you were paying any attention at all you would have noticed that the teachings of the white Christian teachers were very effective. So effective that even today he is not even worried about the few who might somehow stumble across the truth, for he knows how effective he has been. There was a time when he had to use force. There was a time when the white Christian from the New World brought the cross with him, and everyone had to bow down to his god and acknowledge the cross as the symbol of his belief. You either accepted it, or were put to death. There was that time when all nations had to bow to Christians and Muslims through the strength of their swords. Today this is denied by those of us who have copied these same strange philosophies. Both Christians and Muslims have used their philosophies, exposing it to all peoples for their own advantage, so as to subdue and eventually suppress and oppress them into believing in those same philosophies that enslaved them. It worked then, and is still working today.

I have been told many times over, that I should not be teaching white people about the truth concerning the children of Israel or the children of slavery because it's a black thing. Now when you read how effective the lie was, and still is, why should we hide the truth? The people who entertain this thought are lacking in self-confidence, poor in judgment, self-centred and are afraid to face the truth. They are not fit to teach anyone else but themselves. We must remember what is said in **Matthew 28:19-20** **"Go ye therefore, and teach all nations...."**

We as a people are not short on leadership, what we are short on, are leaders with quality. Leaders who are not afraid to face the truth. Leaders who are not too wrapped up in themselves and their egos. Leaders who do not see themselves as little gods. Every black leader talks about blackness all the time. For God's sake we know we are black, what else? We need to know what to do to keep the kids off dope. We need to know what to do to keep them out of jails. We need to train them to be leaders and not followers.

Are we prepared to point in the mirror? Are we prepared to look at the cold hard facts about ourselves?

The white man being the businessman he is, would have been buying pigs in Africa, if there were any for sale. But no, the Muslims were selling our fathers and our mothers, our brothers and our sisters into slavery to the white Christians, whose mind is always working while his money is always turning over. He thinks only of his profit margin. We seem only to see him as the cause of our suffering, but he did not enter into our bedrooms and steal our babies and sell them. He did not hunt us down like dogs in Africa. He did not disrupt our families. He did not take our fathers from the field and away from his family. He did not drag us through the jungles of Western Africa, with the yoke on our necks. He did not tear our babies from the arms of our mothers. He did not rape our mothers and our sisters in Africa. No! He bought us from the real enemy, ourselves. He did not know Africa. He did not know how to find his way into our bedrooms and in our fields. He did not know the way through the streams of our minds. He came with his ship, the Christian cross, and the thirty pieces of silver, and the Judases betrayed us. Yet today these traitors are forgotten and forgiven.

Some Afro Americans today are very proud of a dialect written with the blood of our fathers and our mothers. A dialect created by the Muslims and the Christians in order to communicate on how much our fathers were worth in terms of dollars and cents. This dialect that is now spoken proudly on the lips of the ignorant is called "Swailli." This is one of the tools used against the children of slavery, yet today some of us embrace it.

These same Muslims built warehouses to pack our fathers and our mothers, our sisters and our brothers like sardines waiting for the white man's thirty pieces of silver like Judas. Now in Ghana those same warehouses are called palaces - Slave Palaces. What are the excuses we are hearing from the children of slavery who have adopted the philosophy of Islam today? They are saying that it was white Arabs that came in the jungle and caught our fathers and mothers. Do you believe that there were white Arabs running around in loin cloth in the jungle and in the heat of the Sahara desert?

This statement in itself is a joke, but nobody is laughing. What the white man did to our fathers in the Americas, is nothing in comparison to what the blackman did to his own. If we were not sold by the blackman, we could not have been bought by the white man. We are pointing the finger at the white man, and still running after him and his god. We still seem to be jumping on the bandwagon of skin-colour, and not thinking about truth and our own God. Some of us are wrapped up in our own power structure, seeking ways to justify the wrong that we have done and are doing even now. We first harm ourselves spiritually, and now we are doing it physically. Some teachers are afraid to admit to their congregation that they are wrong, while some are down right ignorant of the truth.

The white Christian can never understand the bible, so he is allowed to make mistakes, but what is very confusing to me, is the fact that black teachers that are wearing the clothing of authority, even calling themselves Israelites, are doing the same things as Christians, or white people who are calling themselves Jews. Some black practitioners are even calling themselves "Israelis" a word created by the white man in 1947-48. I found out also that some Christians are calling themselves Israelites. Black teachers are copying their white counterparts and giving themselves titles such as "Rabbi." The children of slavery should pray for the spirit of understanding and teach others, rather than copy from them. Titles such as "Father" (**Matthew 23:9**) and "Reverend" (**Psalms 111:9**) are understandably used by Christians. Forgive them, for they know not what they do. But why should a person who is suppose to be teaching and leading the children of slavery give himself titles such as "Father, Reverend and Rabbi"

Let us try to understand the meaning of this word **"Rabbi."** The English dictionary gives the meaning as, "a Jew authorized to teach, or to expound Jewish law. The official head of a Jewish congregation." This is a bold face lie. Number one; it is being used in a general term which is wrong. Number two; it is not consistent with what is written in the bible. This is just another way used by the white people who are calling themselves Jews to justify their actions, and because we copy so much from the white man we are now lost in his ignorance, and still crying out how much we hate him. Let him make the mistakes, we have already made too many spiritual mistakes in our generations. The bible says that the word "Rabbi" means "Master", and since we are suppose to be of God, we are suppose to use the bible for spiritual direction and instructions, not the English dictionary. You either take instructions from God, or you follow the tradition of man. There is no in between.

Matthew 23:6-7 "And love the uppermost rooms at feasts, and the chief seats in the synagogues, And greetings in the markets, and to be called of men Rabbi, Rabbi."

The above scripture is a statement from Jesus describing these unworthy men, and at the same time warning His disciples not to do the things that these men were doing. Why would anyone do the opposite today, and still say they are of God? **Verses 8&10** reads "But be not ye called Rabbi: for one is your Master, even Christ; and all ye are brethren. Neither be ye called masters: for one is your Master, even Christ." This was Jesus the Christ talking to His disciples. Are teachers today above the rank of the Christ? The word "Rabbi" is not in the old testament. It was used by people who wanted power over others, the way "Father" is being used by the Christian Catholics.

If you speak to anyone who calls themselves by this name, their excuse would be that John the Baptist was called "Rabbi", so it is O.K. to be called such. The person who uses this excuse should think seriously before using it. First of all, John the Baptist was before the Christ. He came to prepare the way, and the spirit within him was not his own but that of Elijah who came from heaven, bearing in mind that ordinary men cannot go to heaven. Elijah was transformed into a heavenly host. Let's find out first if he went to heaven. **II Kings 2:11** "And it came to pass, as they still went on, and talked, that, behold, there appeared a chariot of fire, and horses of fire, and parted them both asunder; and Elijah went up by a whirlwind into heaven."

John the Baptist was entertaining a spirit from heaven. **Matthew 11:13-14** "For all the prophets and the law prophesied until John. And if ye will receive it, **this is Elias which was for to come.**"

We must understand that this man Elijah was not an ordinary man. Some of you who call yourself by the title bore by this man, should know that after Jesus was baptized by Him (Elijah) and took on the Spirit of the Christ, He then became the Rabbi (Master). This was the handing over of a power the ignorant cannot comprehend. Since you cannot have two Masters on earth, the power of John began to dwindle away, and he began to decrease in status. This is what John the Baptist said in **John 3:29-30** "He that hath the bride is the bridegroom: but the friend of the bridegroom, which standeth and heareth him, rejoiceth greatly because of the bridegroom's voice: this my joy therefore is fulfilled. He must increase, but I must decrease."

If being called "Rabbi" was the right title to be called, why wasn't Peter a "Rabbi?" Or why wasn't Paul a "Rabbi?" Why weren't any of the disciples who were much more qualified called "Rabbis?" Why wasn't Moses, Joshua, Jeremiah, or any of the prophets called "Rabbis?" Why?

The Blackman in the Americas who is claiming to be speaking Hebrew, who is he learning it from? The White man. A pagan and Gentile who adopted the title of being called a Jew, whose real language is Yiddish. What about another example; The bible says in **Psalms 150** that we should praise the Lord our God with every instrument and with DANCE, but Ms Helen White founder of the Seventh Day Adventist says we should not. Do you know that black people prefer to obey Helen White and disobey God Almighty. We must understand that it is O.K. for others to be the way they are, but Israelites must be very careful. We must obey our God, because the instructions are not for Christians, Muslims, or Israelis but Israelites **Psalms 149: 2-3.** We ought to be teachers and not students. Being students have already cost us our dignity. **Hebrews 5:12.**

Believe me, it is better for a white man to teach the doctrine of the blackman, than a black man to teach about another. This knowledge that you are about to obtain in this book, would be about THE WORD, THE ISRAELITES, AND THE DAMNED.

THE BATTLE

With this truth in my mouth
Like honey on my lips
Like a sword in my hand the world I predict
Will crumble and fall - but worst of it all
It would not be quick

I would be there in the wind and the rain
I would be there to ease the pain
Like my fathers before me
Who struggled so hard
I'll be in the battle be it day or night
I would carry this word of truth and of gain
And I'll fight

There is little proof that I may survive
For this word I know lost many a lives
But till these eyes no longer see God's light
And my ears no longer hear a sound
When man can no longer hurt this flesh
Till my body is laid under hollowed ground
And my soul at peace and rest
Till there's no difference between day and night
I'll fight

Till they anoint my body
With spikenard and myrrh
And cover it with a snow white shroud
Till I see Abraham, Isaac and Jacob
And the saints of my father's hand
Till my spirit is rested in Abraham's arm
And paradise embraces my soul at last
Until all this is done and there is no more life
Until then you stiffnecked Israelites
I'll fight.

THROUGH THE EYES
OF A ROMAN
By Tony Castrilli

John 10:14-16 "I am the good shepherd, and know my sheep, and am known of mine. As the Father knoweth me, even so know I the Father: and I lay down my life for the sheep. And other sheep I have, which are not of this fold: them also I must bring, and they shall hear my voice; and there shall be one fold, and one shepherd."

I want to thank the God of my Fathers, the God of Abraham, the God of Isaac and the God of Jacob, that He opened my ears and I heard His voice in 1985. He sent His messenger unto me, teaching the word of truth, which would deliver me from the darkness of this world. His messenger, of course, was an Israelite who knew and spoke of only the doctrine that was given unto the children of Israel. I will proceed in this chapter to prove that no matter what you look like or what kind of past you had, **once you accept the doctrine of Israel** you become part of the fold.

Cornelius, as described in chapter 10 of the Acts of the Apostles, belonged to the Italian band, a centurion and may I also say that he was white (a Roman). An angel of God came to him in a vision. In **Acts 10:5-6** he is told what to do; "And now send men to Joppa, and call for one Simon, whose surname is Peter: He lodgeth with one Simon a tanner, whose house is by the sea side: he shall tell thee what thou oughtest to do."

So here Cornelius is told by an angel of God that he must send for Peter (an Israelite speaking only of the doctrine of Israel) and Peter would tell him what to do to serve the God of Israel. This is very plain and clear. So Cornelius sent two of his household servants and one soldier (three in all) to Joppa for Peter.

Peter was also being prepared for their coming, for while he was praying on the housetop he had a vision. Heaven was opened and a vessel like unto a great sheet knit descended unto him. Wherein were all manner of creeping things (they were unclean). Peter was told to rise; kill and eat.

Acts 10:14-15 "But Peter said, Not so, Lord; for I have never eaten any thing that is common or unclean. And the voice spake unto him again the second time, What God hath cleansed, that call not thou common."

This happened three times and the vessel was received up into heaven. While Peter thought on the vision, the three men were at his gate, and he was told by the Spirit of God to go with these men, doubting nothing.

So here is the picture. Peter, a Blackman, an Israelite, a Jew of the house of Israel was told by the Spirit of Truth to go with these three Gentiles (unclean, not knowing the laws of Israel) and speak unto them what they should do. The next day he and certain brethren (Israelites) departed with the three men for the trip to Caesarea to meet Cornelius. Cornelius was waiting for them, with relatives and close friends. Peter spake in **Acts 10:28** "And he said unto them, Ye know how that it is an unlawful thing for a man that is a Jew to keep company, or come unto one of another nation; but God hath shewed me that I should not call any man common or unclean."

This also erases the Christian myth that you can eat whatever you want and just love God, for in this chapter we are not dealing with food, but it is dealing with a man and his household. "...but God hath shewed me that I should not call **any man common or unclean.**"

Then Cornelius told Peter of his vision, and summed it up and said in **Acts 10:33** "Immediately therefore I sent to thee; and thou hast well done that thou art come. Now therefore are we all here present before God, to hear all things that are commanded thee of God."

Here is Cornelius and his household ready to hear the word of God commanded unto Peter (an Israelite). They would now hear the doctrine of Israel and **only** the doctrine of Israel by a messenger of God. But if this is still not clear, here comes some more proof in the same chapter.

Acts 10:34-36 "Then Peter opened his mouth, and said, Of a truth I perceive that God is no respecter of persons: But in every nation he that feareth him, and worketh righteousness, is accepted with him. The word which God sent unto the children of Israel, preaching peace by Jesus Christ: (he is Lord of all:)"

Peter continues to speak **only of Israel** in **Verse 43** and in **Verse 44**. "While Peter yet spake these words, the Holy Ghost fell on all them which heard the word." What word? If you look back at **Verse 36**, it is very plain. "The word which GOD SENT UNTO THE CHILDREN OF ISRAEL..." In other words, they received the Holy Ghost when they heard the **word sent unto Israel**!

Deuteronomy 5:1-2 "And Moses called all Israel, and said unto them, Hear, O Israel, the statutes and judgments which I speak in your ears this day, that ye may learn them, and keep, and do them. The Lord our God made a covenant with us in Horeb." Those who have ears, shall hear the word of Israel and those who have eyes shall see.

John 1:1 "In the beginning was the Word, and the Word was with God, and the Word was God." **John 1:14** "And the Word was made flesh, and dwelt among us, (and we beheld his glory, the glory as of the only begotten of the Father,) full of grace and truth."

Truth is the word which is the Spirit of the God of Israel. "And the **Word** was made flesh..." Jesus the Christ, taught and spoke only of the doctrine given to His children of Israel. This man Jesus, born a Jew, an Israelite, the Son of David, is the Christ (And the Word was made flesh and dwelt among us...) **John 1:14**.

The "**us**" is the children of Israel, amongst His own! The word was from the beginning! So you see when Peter walked with Jesus the Christ, obviously it was the same **word** that he heard that he also gave freely to Cornelius and his household.

The gift of the Holy Ghost was also given to these Gentiles. They began to speak in tongues (by the Holy Ghost). Then they were baptized by water in the name of the Lord.

I Corinthians 12:13 "For by one Spirit are we all baptized into one body, whether we be Jews or Gentiles, whether we be bond or free; and have been all made to drink into one Spirit."

Romans 15:21 "But as it is written, To whom he was not spoken of, they shall see: and they that have not heard SHALL UNDERSTAND."

There is also the story of Jesus and the centurion. Just picture this: Here's Jesus, an Israelite, born of the fourth son of Jacob, a Jew, a Blackman. He's now being approached by a Roman centurion, a Gentile, a white man, one who does not supposedly know about clean and unclean. It is stated in the book of **Matthew 8:5-8** "And when Jesus was entered into Capernaum, there came unto him a centurion, beseeching him, And saying, Lord, my servant lieth at home sick of the palsy, grievously tormented. And Jesus saith unto him, I will come and heal him. The centurion answered and said, Lord, I am not worthy that thou shouldest come under my roof: BUT SPEAK THE WORD ONLY, AND MY SERVANT SHALL BE HEALED."

"But speak the word only" the word which is life itself, the Spirit of Truth. The word which was given only to the children of Israel out of all the peoples on the face of the earth. For there is no prophet outside of the children of Israel.

Hosea 11:1 "When Israel was a child, then I loved him, and called my son out of Egypt." Here you can see the relationship between God and His people, the Father and His Son.

So, the centurion also said that He wasn't worthy for Jesus to come under his roof. He showed respect and humility towards Israel. The state of his house wasn't possibly right either, for he was living the life of a Gentile (unclean).

The centurion also went on to explain that he is a man under authority having soldiers under him. So, all he has to do is give the command and it is done. So all he's saying is that Jesus has to only give the word and it shall be done, showing much faith and total respect to Israel.

Matthew 8:10 "When Jesus heard it, he marvelled, and said to them that followed, Verily I say unto you, I have not found so great faith, no, not in Israel." So Jesus is saying that this Gentile is showing so much faith that many of His own children in Israel do not have. Again it is a Gentile coming to hear an Israelite, just like Cornelius coming to hear Peter. Jesus goes on to say in **Matthew 8:11** "And I say unto you, That many shall come from the east and west, and shall sit down with Abraham, and Isaac, and Jacob, in the kingdom of heaven."

Look at this verse. It is very plain. All those who come from whatever background, would sit with who? They would sit with Abraham, Isaac and Jacob (Israel). Israel would not go to them, but they would come to be with **Israel**. They would have to know the doctrine of Israel. (There shall be one fold and one Shepherd). I must stress this is the New Testament, **no difference** from the Old Testament. Jesus goes on to say in **Matthew 8:12** "But the children of the kingdom shall be cast out into outer darkness: there shall be weeping and gnashing of teeth."

This is simply explained in the book of **Amos 3:1-2** "Hear this word that the Lord hath spoken against you, O children of Israel, against the whole family which I brought up from the land of Egypt, saying, You only have I known of all the families of the earth: therefore I will punish you for all your iniquities."

This clearly shows that God knows no other people but the children of Israel. So, because of this the Israelites who do not listen, which are disobedient shall suffer and be punished. This is what **Matthew 8:12** is saying. So Jesus goes on to say in **verse 13**, "And Jesus said unto the centurion, Go thy way; and as thou hast believed, so be it done unto thee. And his servant was healed in the selfsame hour." So with the faith the centurion showed in the doctrine of Israel and the respect, and humbleness that He also gave towards Jesus the Christ, his servant was healed in that same hour. **Romans 15:18-19** "For I will not dare to speak of any of those things which Christ hath not wrought by me, to make the Gentiles obedient, by word and deed, Through mighty signs and wonders, by the power of the Spirit of God; SO THAT FROM JERUSALEM, and round about unto Illyricum, I have fully preached the gospel of Christ." So from Jerusalem (the people of Israel) shall the gospel of Christ be preached. To enter, you must know the pass word (the doctrine of Israel).

Revelation 21:10-12 "And he carried me away in the spirit to a great and high mountain, and shewed me that great city, the holy Jerusalem, descending out of heaven from God, Having the glory of God: and her light was like unto a stone most precious, even like a jasper stone, clear as crystal; And had a wall great and high, and had twelve gates, and at the gates twelve angels, and names written thereon, which are the names of the TWELVE TRIBES OF THE CHILDREN OF ISRAEL:" Jerusalem here is not a physical city. It is where the God of Israel puts His name. The gates (entrances) are all Israel. In order to get in you must know the **password**! Revelation is what is to come.

SCATTERING OF ISRAEL

II Kings 17:6&18 "In the ninth year of Hoshea the king of Assyria took Samaria, and carried Israel away into Assyria, and placed them in Halah and in Habor by the river of Gozan, and in the cities of the Medes. **Verse 18** "Therefore the Lord was very angry with Israel, and removed them out of his sight: there was none left but the tribe of Judah only."

II Kings 24:10&16 "At that time the servants of Nebuchadnezzar king of Babylon came up against Jerusalem, and the city was besieged. **Verse 16** "And all the men of might, even seven thousand, and craftsmen and smiths a thousand, all that were strong and apt for war, even them the king of Babylon brought captive to Babylon."

In the year 597 B.C. (March 16) Jerusalem is taken by Babylon. The kingdom of Judah would spend 70 years in Babylon (more scattering and dispersing). Judah would return for the coming of the Christ. **James 1:1** "James, a servant of God and of the Lord Jesus Christ, TO THE TWELVE TRIBES WHICH ARE SCATTERED ABROAD, greeting."

The generations of God's chosen from Abraham to our Lord Jesus Christ is listed in **Matthew 1**. In the year 70 A.D. the removal of the Israelites from the land is completed with the Romans burning down of Jerusalem. The Jews (Israelites) are taken as slaves and scattered, never to return.

Zechariah 7:14 "But I scattered them with a whirlwind among all the nations whom they knew not. Thus the land was desolate after them, that no man passed through **nor returned:** for they laid the pleasant land desolate."

With this all being done about two thousand years ago, there's been a lot of mixing of people with the Israelites. You cannot tell by the physical appearance anymore. Many people would be surprised (or shocked) to know what their great-great grandparents looked like. Only with the children of slavery (in the Americas) do we know of a certainty that they are Israelites by birth. Read **Deuteronomy 28:68** "And the Lord shall bring thee into Egypt again with ships, by the way whereof I spake unto thee, **Thou shalt see it no more again:**

and there ye shall be sold unto your enemies for bondmen and bondwomen, and no man shall buy you."

Jeremiah 30:10 & 11 "Therefore fear thou not, O my servant Jacob, saith the Lord; neither be dismayed, O Israel: for, lo, I will save thee from afar, and thy seed from the land of their captivity; and Jacob shall return, and shall be in rest, and be quiet, and none shall make him afraid. For I am with thee, saith the Lord to save thee: though I make a full end of all nations whither I have scattered thee, yet will I not make a full end of thee: but I will correct thee in measure, and will not leave thee altogether unpunished."

In **Verse 10** it states that the God of Israel will gather His children (Israel) and their seed from the oppressor. The seed being passed on by a man of Israel from one generation to the next. And Israel shall be saved. In **Verse 11** it also states that the nations in which Israel has been scattered shall be punished. Yet those who return to the God of Israel (knowing and doing according to the doctrine) shall rest.

Jeremiah 31:33 & 34 "But this shall be the covenant that I will make with the house of Israel; After those days, saith the Lord, I will put my law in their inward parts, and write it in their hearts; and will be their God, and they shall be my people. And they shall teach no more every man his neighbour, and every man his brother, saying, Know the Lord: for they shall all know me, from the least of them unto the greatest of them, saith the Lord: for I will forgive their iniquity, and I will remember their sin no more." "I will put my law in their inward parts..." The word given to the House of Israel shall be written within the individuals whom the Lord God of Israel shall call. And Israel shall be forgiven their sin and iniquity. Once you accept the doctrine of Israel and live it, no matter what you look like (as shown in the scattering) you become one of the family of God.

Revelation 7:4 "And I heard the number of them which were sealed: and there were sealed an hundred and forty and four thousand of all the tribes of the children of Israel."

Isaiah 45:17 "But Israel shall be saved in the Lord with an everlasting salvation: ye shall not be ashamed nor confounded world without end."

Luke 1:33 "And he shall reign over the house of Jacob FOR EVER; and of his kingdom there shall be NO END."

It is stated in the book of **Ezekiel 47:22** "And it shall come to pass, that ye shall divide it by lot for an inheritance unto you, and to the strangers that sojourn among you, which shall beget children among you: and they shall be unto you as born in the country among the children of Israel; they shall have inheritance with you among the tribes of Israel."

I am of Italian heritage, white in my appearance, an Israelite from head to toe. I am a man of truth as all the forefathers of Israel stood for. Solomon, who was blessed with so much wisdom, knowledge and understanding, said to do whatever you can to get the truth. Once you have it, give the word freely to those who have ears to hear.

Why is it so difficult to accept by both black and white alike, that God, His Heavenly Hosts, His Prophets, His Saints and His Apostles, except Titus were all black, even though the bible is loaded with proof? Yet on the other hand, silently everyone black, white, oriental, the entire world accepts the white long-haired picture as being Jesus when there is absolutely no proof anywhere.

Proverbs 23:23 "Buy the truth, and sell it not; also wisdom, and instruction, and understanding."

There is no truth outside of THE HOUSE OF ISRAEL and THE ISRAELITES. Not white-skinned Israelis. NONE.

THE SEVENTH TRUMPET

Sing a song - Sing a song both loud and clear
Sing a song oh Israel to our God the one to fear
Music is of seven letters
One for each day of the week
Our God alone is seven Israel
If you don't know this learn to seek

When you add the complete package
By no coincidence there are twelve you see
The number of the tribes of Israel
God's chosen for eternity

So the structure of music
Is not of man you see - Not of man at all
For it was with our God and His hosts
From the beginning during creation
Before Lucifer's fall

The world now has received this knowledge
Knowing both right and wrong
Music is such a powerful tool
To bring together even the lie
But not for long

I know this would make the world so mad
To know even music belongs to us
There to worship our God of Israel in truth
Just look at the facts
It's a must

But don't fret Israel for the prophecy must unfold
Our God He has it all laid out
144,000 souls to be sealed
Then the seventh trumpet will sound
With a shout

As it was in the beginning
It also shall be in the end
God's chosen shall sing a new song unto Him
But the rest shall be cut off
Praise to the God of Israel

THE PHILOSOPHICAL BACKGROUND OF THE ISRAELIS
By Michael Hinds

We live in a world today in which the **TRUTH** is no longer popular. In fact, to tell the truth today, could get us in a great deal of trouble. Therefore, deception, to varying degrees, has become the new world order. One aspect of deception is to conceal the facts of history, so that it might appear that one is not openly lying, but since some of us still seek and speak the truth, it would only be a matter of time before the whole truth is revealed. One such revelation involves the difference between the Israelites and the Israelis. Some of us would consider this subject to be very controversial, therefore my statements will be substantiated with verifiable facts.

We must understand very clearly that there is no greater authority on TRUTH than the holy bible and specifically, the authorized or King James Version. When the holy scriptures were first being written, there were no other books intended for mass circulation available anywhere. Do not be fooled by "books" like the Egyptian "Pyramid Texts", Coffin Texts", or "Book of the Dead". These were not books in the true sense of the word as we know it today; but rather symbols engraved or painted on the inner walls of the Pyramids. Only the initiated few, chiefly the priesthood and the elite, including the King (Pharaoh) were exposed to such "Books". The High Priest or Hierophant was the Keeper of the Sacred Word. He supervised the teaching of the initiates from the symbols on the walls of the pyramids. Each symbol represented a story, which could fill the pages of a book. All teaching was orally and in secret, never to be revealed to anyone. Of course, one could argue that the scriptures had to be taught orally at first until the scribes were able to make several copies. But the main difference was that ALL ISRAELITES were exposed to the teachings of the scriptures, with nothing hidden or secret.

Therefore, as seekers of TRUTH, we must be willing to scrutinize ALL writers of history, especially those of the eighteenth and nineteenth centuries, when the spiritual degradation of humanity was clearly manifested. Prejudices, fears and hatred, fuelled by a sense of great inadequacy when confronted with the truth, took precedence over facts and an hidden agenda was formulated.

There must however, be a fixed standard by which all things can be measured. This standard is readily available in the holy scriptures. The scriptures document the origins of our universe and our life with profound accuracy. They also give an historical perspective of civilization from the beginning right up to the first one hundred years of this present era. The events shaping the rest of our duration on this planet may also be found in the scriptures, specifically the prophecies. All this show the power and completeness of the bible, making it the sole authority on TRUTH among humanity. It even became symbolic with our justice system while that system functioned. Many may dispute these facts, but none can ever prove them wrong.

FOUNDATION

Let me state emphatically that there is absolutely nothing in common between an Israelite and an Israeli. The difference is like black and white. The Israelites consist of twelve tribes according to **Exodus 1:1-4**, "Now these are the names of the children of Israel, which came into Egypt: every man and his household came with Jacob.

Rueben, Simeon, Levi, and Judah. Issachar, Zebulun, and Benjamin, Dan, and Naphtali, Gad, and Asher." Joseph made up the twelveth.

The Israelis consists of two tribes. Ten to twenty percent are Edomites which are the children of Esau who was called Edom in the book of **Genesis 36:1**, "Now these are the generations of Esau, who is called Edom."

The remaining eighty to ninety percent are known as **Khazars** or **Khazarians.**

THE KHAZARS
THEIR HISTORICAL BACKGROUND

The year is 450 A.D. and one of Europe's barbaric tribes is beginning to show signs of restlessness. This tribe is called the **KHAZARS** (Chazars). Within the next two hundred years, the Khazars would form Eastern Europe's largest and most powerful kingdom.

They would rule supreme for about 200 years, ranking in power with the Muslim Caliphate and the Byzantine Empire. Their kingdom, of approximately one million square miles bordered the Aral sea on the east; Kiev and the Ukrainian Steppes on the west; the Caucasus mountain and the Black Sea on the south; and the Ural mountain on the north.

It is quite obvious from the foregoing historical facts that Khazaria represented a very important period in European history. Why is it that we cannot read about it from the history text in our schools? It is very uncharacteristic of the Europeans not to flaunt their heritage. They have gone to great lengths to invent ridiculous adjectives like "Caucasoid" and nouns such as "Indo-European" and "Aryan" in order to imply Caucasian, when the facts proved otherwise. So why is Khazaria a secret? It is rather strange indeed, since there is so much written about Attila the Hun, even movies made about him and his people.

The Huns lasted less than 100 years from *ca.* 372-455 A.D. while the Khazars lasted about five hundred years (500) and followed the Huns by about two hundred years. They ruled supreme for two hundred out of those five hundred years. In those days the Caspian Sea as we know it today, was called the Sea of the Khazars.

It would be next to impossible not to know of the Khazars, in fact, without their valour, Europe would have probably been one hundred percent Muslim today. It is inconceivable that all these important and historical facts would go unmentioned by proud Europeans and their historians. These same people who want the world to believe, and to some extent have the world believing, that God is, or was a Caucasian and that they are from the family of God.

They were so brilliant in conning the entire world, yet never printed this history in their text books? This is definitely a mystery!

THEIR SPIRITUAL BACKGROUND

If we read the book of Ephesians, we will discover that the Gentiles had the spirit of the air and not the spirit of God. Now they have taken the authority, and are corrupting the world with their strange philosophy, especially the children of slavery, who do not even know their God. Everybody else's god is important except their own. Consequently, today the children of slavery suffer greatly from the same spirit of the air the Gentiles had!

Let us now examine very carefully the genealogy of the Khazars. Since this matter is so important, we shall allow the Kagan or King to inform us. King Joseph corresponded with a Spanish Israelite named Hasdai Ibn Shaprut sometime between 954 and 961 A.D. (*Manuscripts of this correspondence may be seen in the Library of Christ Church at Oxford, England and in the Leningrad Public Library in Leningrad, Russia.*)

Hasdai was the chief minister of the Caliph of Cordoba, who was Abd-al-Rahman III. At that time Cordoba was the splendour of Moorish Spain (a mixture of Muslims and Israelites known as black Jews), and was the main centre of European Culture.

In his letter to Hasdai, King Joseph stated that he was from the line of Japheth, from the seed of Togarmah, Japheth's grandson. He further stated that Togarmah, who was the brother of **ASHKENAZ**, had ten sons and the Khazars represented the seventh son. With his own lips this King had given the root of his being and the lineage of his offspring. Let us now see what the scriptures have to say about Japheth and Togarmah in the book of **Genesis 10: 2-5**. " The sons of Japheth; Gomer, and Magog, and Madai, and Javan, and Tubal, and Meshech, and Tiras. And the sons of Gomer; Ashkenaz, and Riphat, and Togarmah. And the sons of Javan; Elishah, and Tarshish, Kittim, and Dodanim.

By these were the Isles of the Gentiles divided in their lands; everyone after his tongue, after their families, in their nations."

As they would have said today; "out of the horse's mouth, can only come a confession." According to the king of the Khazars, his tribe descended from the family of Magog. Let's continue in the Holy Bible to see what God has to say about the forefathers of the Khazars - MAGOG, GOG, GOMER, AND TOGARMAH. Read **Ezekiel 38:2-3**. "Son of man, set thy face against Gog, the land of Magog, the chief prince of Meshech and Tubal, and prophesy against him, And say, Thus saith the Lord God; Behold, I am against thee, O Gog, the chief prince of Meshech and Tubal:"

The enemy of God has now been identified in the scriptures.**Verse 6** "Gomer, and all his bands; the house of Togarmah of the north quarters, and all his bands: and many people with thee." **Verse 8** "After many days thou shall be visited: in the latter years thou shalt come into the land that is brought back from the sword, and is gathered out of many people, against the mountains of Israel, which have been always waste: but it is brought forth out of the nations, and they shall dwell safely all of them."

We are seeing today the revelation of this very important statement, which we have just read, happening in the land some people called Israel in 1947-48.

Verse 10-12 "Thus saith the Lord God; It shall also come to pass, that at the same time shall things come into thy mind, and thou shalt think an evil thought: And thou shalt say, I will go up to the land of unwalled villages; I will go to them that are at rest, that dwell safely, all of them dwelling without walls, and having neither bars or gates, To take a spoil, and to take a prey; to turn thine hand upon the desolate places that are now inhabited, and upon the people that are gathered out of the nations, which have gotten cattle and goods, that dwell in the midst of the land." **Verse 14-15** "Therefore, son of man, prophesy and say unto Gog, Thus saith the Lord GOD; In that day when my people of Israel dwelleth safely, shalt thou not know it? And thou shalt come from thy place out of the north parts, thou, and many people with thee, all of them riding upon horses, a great company, and a might army:"

Mighty army is correct, just take a look at Israel today. We must also read **Ezekiel chapter 39**, paying special attention to the following scriptures: **Verses 1-6** "Therefore, thou son of man, prophesy against Gog, and say, Thus saith the Lord GOD; Behold, **I am against thee, O Gog,** the chief prince of Meshech and Tubal: And I will turn thee back, and leave but the sixth part of thee, and will cause thee to come up from the north parts, and will bring thee upon the mountains of Israel: And I will smite thy bow out of thy left hand, and will cause thine arrows to fall out of thy right hand. Thou shalt fall upon the mountains of Israel, thou, and all thy bands, and the people that is with thee: I will give thee unto the ravenous birds of every sort, and to the beasts of the field to be devoured. Thou shalt fall upon the open field: for I have spoken it, saith the Lord GOD. And I will send a fire on Magog, and among them that dwell carelessly in the isles: and they shall know that I am the Lord." **Verse 11** "And it shall come to pass in that day, that I will give unto Gog a place there of graves in Israel, the valley of the passengers on the east of the sea: and it shall stop the noses of the passengers: and there shall they bury Gog and all his multitude: and they shall call it the valley of Hamongog."

As an Israelite, it is not my place to question what the Almighty God had said in his Holy Words. These scriptures indicate the sign of the end.

To conclude read **Revelation 20:7-10** "And when the thousand years are expired, Satan shall be loosed out of his prison, And shall go out to deceive the nations which are in the four quarters of the earth, Gog and Magog, to gather them together to do battle: the number of whom is as the sand of the sea. And they went up on the breadth of the earth, and compassed the camp of the saints about, and the beloved city: and fire came down from God out of heaven, and devoured them. And the devil that deceived them was cast into the lake of fire and brimstone, where the beast and the false prophet are, and shall be tormented day and night for ever and ever." Note that GOG and MAGOG are one of the same, i.e. same family. Gog is the king or ruler, while Magog represents the people over whom he rules. These scriptures are very clear indeed. God calls His enemies by name. It is very important to note that God's enemies will come mainly from the NORTH, during the latter days, settle in the land of ancient Israel from among many nations, to do evil. Our God shall destroy these heathens and His name shall be magnified throughout this world forever.

THE EVOLUTION OF JUDAISM

Like all European nations at the time, the Khazars were pagans. However, ca. 740 A.D. King Bulan initiated the conversion of his kingdom to a new and different philosophy. Before the conversion, the Kagan invited representatives of Christianity, Islam and the Israelites to discuss the three doctrines. It was unanimously agreed, in response to the Kagan's question, that the doctrine of the Israelites was closest to the truth. The king changed his name to become King Obadiah and invited Pharisees (Israelites) from Babylonia to teach the Khazarians from the **Mishna** and the **Talmud**. The philosophy of the Talmud is called **Talmudism** and the Khazars tried to adopt this doctrine as their new philosophy. The Khazars remained pagans, only changing philosophies. They displayed much hope but very little understanding, especially of spiritual matters. Eventually, they had to invent their own brand of Talmudism, which they named **JUDAISM**. The word "Judaism" cannot be found in the writings of the Prophets of old, neither is it found anywhere in the Holy Bible. Therefore, it **cannot** be of God. It is a new name created by the Khazars and has **nothing** to do with the children of Judah (Israelites). Just like others who use the name "Christian", but have **absolutely nothing** to do with Christ. Man created the word "Judaism", then placed it in a dictionary to mean "from or of Jews." This is a **lie**! The Romans also found the word "Christian" and placed it in a dictionary to mean "follower of Christ." This is also a **lie**! **All the followers of Christ were Israelites**, according to the word of God.

Judaism, therefore, is a misunderstanding or perversion of the customs of the ancient Israelites, as practised by the Khazars. This pagan philosophy has evolved from the

Khazarian Council of Mainz in 1000 A.D. Obviously then, the customs of the Israelites were **never** practised by the Khazars. Let us see what God has to say regarding pagan philosophies and traditions. For proof read **Matthew 15:1-9** with special reference to **Verses 4-9**. "For God commanded, saying, Honour thy father and mother: and, He that curseth father or his mother, let him die the death. But ye say, Whosoever shall say to his father and mother, It is a gift, by whatsoever thou mightest be profited by me; And honour not his father or his mother, he shall be free. Thus have ye made the commandment of God of none effect by your tradition. Ye hypocrites, well did Esaias prophesy of you, saying, This people draweth nigh unto me with their mouth, and honoureth me with their lips; but their heart is far from me. But in vain do they worship me, teaching for doctrines the commandments of men." Mark makes the same point in **Mark 7:1-13**, while in **Colossians 2:8**, Paul warns, "Beware lest any man spoil you through philosophy and vain deceit, after the tradition of men, after the rudiments of the world, and not after Christ." With these scriptures in mind, now we shall prove how Judaism is a pagan philosophy and represents the tradition of man.

The Kagan selected his best scholars to study and report,. but they, being "blind", could not discern the truth of the Talmud. During the tenth century, the Khazars would be attacked by the Vikings or Norsemen from the West and the Rus or Varangians from the East. These same Vikings would become the Scandinavians, while the Rus would become the Russians. Between the 11th and 12th centuries, the Khazars would cease to exist as a nation. They lost their nationality to become a part of Russia, Ukrainia, Rumania, Hungary, Austria, Czechoslovakia, Poland, Germany, and Lithuania. But their faith in this newly founded Judaism remained strong. In addition, by combining East German dialects with Slavonic and Baltic words and their own Turkish language, the Khazars produced a new dialect called **YIDDISH**. Therefore, with a common tongue and a common philosophy the Khazars created a unique culture. It is important to note that Yiddish is **NOT** Hebrew and should not be confused with the language of the ancient Israelites. There are many fools who are following in this path.

The destruction of Khazaria exposed the Khazars to the cultures of Western Europe, especially the SPANISH ISRAELITES or SEPHARDIM. For many centuries, they attempted to ride on the coat-tails of the Sephardim. They did not assume the nationality of their new countries, but rather referred to themselves as YIDDISH or "Jews." The name "Jew" may have been a nickname, but today it has erroneously assumed very strong implications. One leading Khazarian priest was Gershom ben Judah (960-1030). Gershom saw the need for an international brotherhood of Khazarians, since they were lacking that rich heritage of the Spanish Israelites. So he borrowed from the Christians and their culture of Feudal Europe and convened the Council of Mainz (Germany) in 1000 A.D. Along with the leading Khazarian priests, Gershom approved extreme *takkanas* or decrees, which even conflicted with both the Talmud and the Torah. It was strictly a case of the blind leading the blind. Gershom simply could not discern the truth; so he applied only secular reasoning, which had nothing to do with God. The final product would be a socioeconomic and political blue-print for self-government of the Khazarian community, within their respective countries. This blue-print would also form the basis of what is known today as Judaism: the European Talmudic Code.

Later, another Khazarian, named Shlomo Itzhaki or RASHI (1040-1105) a so-called rabbi, would add the main philosophical dimension to Gershom's Talmudic Code. At first Rashi tried to teach from the Babylonian Talmud, but he just could not understand it. Thus Rashi started to write his own interpretation of the Talmud, even though the Talmud specifically warns that one who interprets a biblical verse is a LIAR, and one who elaborates is a BLASPHEMER. Rashi would produce a European version of the Talmud, written with much warmth and love, just like the Christianized versions of the bible today. Naturally, the Christians of Rashi's era found his philosophy appealing. Later Martin Luther would be influenced by Rashi's Judaic writing to spawn his Reformation. From 1100-1130 A.D. French and

German Khazars would continue to add to the perversion of ancient Israelite customs, just like the Christians have done today. These Yiddish scholars were named TOSAFISTS, which means "to add".

With the brilliant literature coming from the Sephardim or Spanish Israelites and the shallow works of the Khazarian Tosafists, some conflict was inevitable. As always it would be the one producing the inferior quality who would complain strongest. In the thirteenth century, the French Tosafists criticized the Spanish Sephardim for not stipulating the sources of their reasoning. These Israelites were accustomed to clear, logical, sound reasoning and lived in an environment of extremely high intellectuals, unlike the Khazars. Therefore, there was absolutely no need for listing references. There were no references in their book, the holy bible. The Israelites wrote mainly from inspiration, knowing that there are no references for "original" thought. The Khazarian Tosafists, on the other hand, listed, as is common today, a reference appendix as proof. Being shallow, they had to justify every statement, so they would reference each other for credibility. Of course, referencing someone else does not make a statement correct or valid, it might only serve to show the extent of the folly, much as it does today.

However, Judaism continued to evolve and Jacob ben Asher (1270-1343), a Khazarian Tosafist, would later produce his version of the Europeanized Talmud which he called the "FOUR ROWS". It combined French and German learning with interpreted Sephardim teaching. It heralded the full introduction of Judaism as a product of thirteenth century Europe. This European pagan philosophy would later be amplified in the Khazarian ghettos of Eastern Europe.

Between 1300 and 1500, a group of dull and mediocre Yiddish scholars called the MAHARILS would condense Khazarian culture into a formal and conforming system. Jacob Molin (1360-1427) was one such man. Every aspect of Khazarian life became a ritual and was standardized, from birth to death. Even the dress code for certain men became law: a long black coat and a big, ridiculous, black hat. Then to imitate the Israelites, they would artificially curl their long, straight hair, since they lacked the natural black, woolly hair of the Israelites.

Thus the Talmud became a degraded document in the hands of the Khazars and Judaism evolved. It became a code of Khazarian absurdities and mundane cultural rituals. We can even see the Khazarian today engaging in such rituals as he jerks his body to and fro in a sexual frenzy, against an old, dilapidated wall. Such practices by the Khazars has allowed for their stereotyping and also they being seen as a symbol of EVIL. Therefore, the so-called "Jews" of today should not be confused with the descendants of the biblical Israelites. Let us go to the scriptures to see what GOD has to say about this great perversion by these Khazarian descendants. **Revelation 2:9**, "I know thy works, and tribulation, and poverty, (but thou art rich) and I know the blasphemy of them which say they are Jews, and are not, but are the synagogue of Satan;" and **3:9**, "Behold, I will make them of the synagogue of Satan, which say they are Jews, and are not, but do lie; behold, I will make them to come and worship before thy feet, and to know that I have loved thee," should put this matter to rest forever.

THE RESTORATION

In the late 19th century the Khazarians or Yiddish would start their "exodus" from Eastern Europe to Western Europe and the Americas. In the U.S.A. they would become very successful, especially in the motion picture industry. They would own all but two of the major Hollywood film production companies. However, the Yiddish or East European had not given up trying to restore their Kingdom.

In 1916 the British, fighting a losing war with the French against the Germans, solicited the aid of the Yiddish. The Khazarian descendants were asked to use their influence to bring the Americans'into the war on the side of the allies. In return the British promised to give Palestine to the Khazars for their homeland. On April 6, 1917, the United States declared war on Germany. On November 2, 1917 the British issued the Balfour Declaration as their part of the deal with the Khazars.

Thirty years later, the United Nations would issue its Partition Resolution on November 29, 1947. The following year the Khazarians would finally have what they called their homeland, where they would join themselves with the remnant from the tribe of **ESAU**, the **EDOMITES** and together called themselves **ISRAELIS**.

On March 12, 1917 the Yiddish or so-called Jews would bring about the Bolshevik Revolution in Russia. Later Stalin would end the Bolshevik rule by June 1930. But even Stalin, a Gentile, was married to a Yiddish woman.

In 1918 the Yiddish-dominated German Social democratic Party, overthrew the Kaiser and proclaimed Germany a Socialist Republic on November 9, 1918. Suddenly, in 1933, Hitler rose up to end the Khazarian or Yiddish rule a year later.

In 1919, the Khazarian Bela Kun imposed a communist regime on Hungary. After three months of chaos, he was quickly deposed. But in 1945, Hungary would once again feel the wrath of another Yiddish dictatorship. This time Matya Rakosi would be installed as communist boss. The communist Khazars would also rule Poland and Czechoslovakia.

EDOMITES
Identity and Location

As mentioned before, we know that Edom descended from Shem and that the Edomites (descendants of Edom) comprise less than 20% of the Israeli population. But it would appear that this small segment of Semitic lineage is cleverly used, along with Judaism, to imply the Semitic origin of all Israelis. We have, therefore, neutralized this delicate matter, which has been a mystery to many, by utilizing the TRUTH. Now let us turn to the scriptures to prove the identity of Edom.

First, let us read **Genesis 25:21-30**: "And Isaac intreated the Lord for his wife, because she was barren: and the Lord was intreated of him, and Rebekah his wife conceived. And the children struggled together within her; and she said, If it be so, why am I thus? And she went to inquire of the Lord. And the Lord said unto her, Two nations are in thy womb, and two manner of people shall be separated from thy bowels; and the one people shall be stronger than the other people; and the elder shall serve the younger. And when her days to be delivered were fulfilled, behold, there were twins in her womb. And the first came out red, all over like an hairy garment; and they called his name Esau. And after that came his brother out, and his hand took hold on Esau's heel; and his name was called Jacob:" **Verses 29-30** states, "And Jacob sod pottage: and Esau came from the field, and he was faint: And Esau said to Jacob, Feed me, I pray thee, with that same red pottage; for I am faint: therefore was his name called Edom."

We will note that there are two different types of people within Rebekah's womb, so that separation was made by God Himself before birth. Also, we must understand that a normal, healthy, "black" baby is not usually red at birth, but most "white" babies are. In addition, the Hebrews called what was red Edom, so Esau was called Edom because of his red appearance. Unlike Jacob and the others, Esau, similar to any Caucasian who has been exposed to too much direct sunlight, turned reddish (faint) while in the field. Since we are on this topic of colour, let us clear up some additional confusion, using TRUTH and COMMON SENSE.

Many Christian teachers have erroneously applied this same principle of Edom meaning red to Adam. But there is nothing in common between Edom and Adam. Adam means human (HUEMAN) or black man. Since hue means colour and Adam was made from the PUREST and RICHEST soil, i.e. the BLACKEST, then common sense would dictate that Adam would have to be a BLACK MAN. According to the Holy Bible, God created Adam in His IMAGE and LIKENESS, so any comments on Adam's appearance would also be a comment on God's appearance at the time. Therefore, we must be sure to speak the TRUTH, at least regarding this matter. Furthermore, we all know that the Caucasian cannot produce the melanin required to give the skin its colour and must remain colourless. The sun-tan is only a reflection of damaged skin. Without getting too complicated, however, there are two other words which share a common origin with "human" - "humus" and "humble."

The linguist may want to research the Latin, Greek and Hebrew origins, but humus is the black organic portion of the soil which is essential for its fertility. Humble means ranking low in a hierarchy, i.e. of the earth.

Now back to Edom. Let us read **Genesis 27:11** "And Jacob said to Rebekah his mother, Behold, Esau my brother is a hairy man, and I am a smooth man:" **Verses 15-16** read, "And Rebekah took goodly raiment of her eldest son Esau, which were with her in the house, and put them upon Jacob her younger son: And she put the skins of the kids of the goats upon his hands, and upon the smooth of his neck." It is quite clear that not only is Jacob smooth and "hairless" like most black men, but he had to disguise himself with the straight, long hair of the goat. There should be no confusion now about these two different men.

Edom would later settle in Mount Seir, to the south of Judah as stated in **Genesis 32:3**, "And Jacob sent messengers before him to Esau his brother unto the land of Seir, the country of Edom." Later yet Edom would refuse passage through his country to his Israelite cousins en route to the Promised Land from Egypt. **Numbers 20:14-21** says, "And Moses sent messengers from Kadesh unto the king of Edom, Thus saith thy brother Israel, Thou knowest all the travail that hath befallen us: How our fathers went down into Egypt, and we have dwelt in Egypt a long time; and the Egyptians vexed us, and our fathers: And when we cried unto the Lord, he heard our voice, and sent an angel, and hath brought us forth out of Egypt: and, behold, we are in Kadesh, a city in the uttermost of thy border: Let us pass, I pray thee, through thy country: we will not pass through the fields, or through the vineyards, neither will we drink of the water of the wells: we will go by the king's high way: we will not turn to the right hand or to the left, until we have passed thy borders. And Edom said unto him, Thou shalt not pass by me, lest I come out against thee with the sword. And the children of Israel said unto him, We will go by the highway, and if I and my cattle drink of thy water, then I will pay for it: I will only, without doing anything else, go through on my feet. And he said, Thou shalt not go through. And Edom came out against him with much people, and with a strong hand.

Thus Edom refused to give Israel passage though his border; wherefore Israel turned away from him."

Finally, Edom would join with the Babylonian army of Nebuchadnezzar to attack the Israelites and even occupy their land in southern Judea, which was then called IDUMEA. Now let us see what GOD has to say about Edom.

EDOM AND GOD

In the book of **Malachi 1:2-4** GOD says, "I have loved you, saith the Lord. Yet ye say, Wherein hast thou loved us? Was not Esau Jacob's brother? saith the Lord: yet I loved Jacob, **And I hated Esau,** and laid his mountains and his heritage waste for the dragons of the wilderness. Whereas Edom saith, We are impoverished, but we will return and build the desolate places; thus saith the Lord of hosts, They shall build, but I will throw down; and they shall call them, The border of wickedness, and, The people against whom the Lord hath indignation for ever." In the book of **Ezekiel** GOD'S judgment against Edom has been prophesied in **chapter 35**. Special attention should be paid to the following: **Verse 2** says, "Son of man, set thy face against mount Seir, and prophesy against it." **Verse 4-5** says, "I will lay thy cities waste, and thou shalt be desolate, and thou shalt know that I am the Lord. Because thou hast had a perpetual hatred, and hast shed the blood of the children of Israel by the force of the sword in the time of their calamity, in the time that their iniquity had an end." **Verses 7-9** say, "Thus will I make mount Seir most desolate, and cut off from it him that passeth out and him that returneth. And I will fill his mountains with his slain men in thy hills, and in thy valleys, and in all thy rivers, shall they fall that are slain with the sword. I will make thee perpetual desolations, and thy cities shall not return: and ye shall know that I am the Lord." **Verse 12** reads, "And thou shalt know that I am the Lord, and that I have heard all thy blasphemies which thou hast spoken against the mountains of Israel, saying, They are laid desolate, they are given to us to consume." **Verse 15** states, "As thou didst rejoice at the inheritance of the house of Israel, because it was desolate, so will I do unto thee: thou shalt be desolate, O mount Seir, and all Idumea, even all of it: and they shall know that I am the LORD."

In the book of **Obadiah**, note what GOD has to say about Edom in **Verse 2**, "Behold, I have made thee small among the heathen: thou art greatly despised." While **Verses 10-16** tells us of Edom's injustice against the Israelites and the prophesy of their curse. "For thy violence against thy brother Jacob shame shall cover thee, and thou shalt be cut off for ever. In the day that thou stoodest on the other side, in the day that the strangers carried away captive his forces, and foreigners entered into his gates, and cast lots upon Jerusalem, even thou wast as one of them. But thou shouldest not have looked on the day of thy brother in the day that he became a stranger; neither shouldest thou have rejoice over the children of Judah in the day of their destruction; neither shouldest thou have spoken proudly in the day of distress. Thou shouldest not have entered into the gate of my people in the day of their calamity; yeah, thou shouldest not have looked on their affliction in the day of their calamity, nor have laid hands their substance in the day of their calamity; Neither shouldest thou have stood in the crossway, to cut off those of his that did escape; neither shouldest thou have delivered up those of his that did remain in the day of distress. For the day of the Lord is near upon all the heathen: as thou hast done, it shall be done unto thee: thy reward shall return upon thine own head. For as ye have drunk upon my holy mountain, so shall all the heathen drink continually, yea, they shall drink, and they shall shallow down, and they shall be as though they had not been."

CONCLUSION

One thing we have learnt is that history never lies. We have learnt that the so-called Jew is not a Jew at all, but a Gentile. We have learnt that this Gentile has descended from the family of GOG and MAGOG and not from the House of Jacob. We have also learnt that Edom has joined with this Gentile to deliberately pervert the word of God, mocked Him continually and they have therefore become God's biggest enemy. Woe unto them! Next we shall take a look at the real Israelites, God's Chosen People.

First, let us understand who is a JEW. A Jew is an ISRAELITE from the tribe of Judah. The Israelites consist of twelve tribes and Judah is the fourth. All Jews are Israelites, but all Israelites are not Jews. The Jews represent the rulers of the House of Israel, or Nation of Israel. Do not forget that ISRAEL was a man called JACOB, who had twelve sons which were called Israelites. Contrary to popular opinion, Moses was not a Jew but a Levite, the third son or tribe, neither was Abraham a Jew. He was a Hebrew and not an Israelite. Now that we have cleared up some of the confusion, we shall again take the guided tour of history, led by the TRUTH to learn of the real Israelites.

By now we should have a very good understanding of the Israeli and also of a Jew. So the next time a Christian preacher tries to explain scriptures pertaining to the Israelites by referencing the Israelis, we would know what to do. Before we start to deal with the Israelites, let us pause and think for a while.

We have all seen, or are aware of the awesome power of the Israelis. Their military might is easily the most effective in the world today. In addition, they are backed by the most powerful economic and military system on earth. So why don't they called themselves Israelites? Why skirt the issue? What's in a name? To call themselves Israelites would mean a direct confrontation with GOD Himself and we know who would lose. This issue is one of REAL POWER-SPIRITUAL POWER, and not petty nuclear bombs. So when everything is said and done, even Lucifer with all his might, knows his place.

The Israelites descended from Jacob; while the Khazars descended from Japheth and the Edomites from Esau. The Israelites originated from North-Eastern Africa; while the Khazars originated from South-Eastern Europe and the Edomites from the Southern Palestine/Jordan area.

The Israelites have black skin, according to the Holy Bible, with woolly hair, a big broad nose and thick, fleshy lips. The Israelis have white skin, blue eyes mostly, long straight hair, usually blonde, thin lips (if any) and a straight, thin nose. The Israelites spoke Egyptian, Hebrew, Aramaic and later Greek, Roman, Spanish, various West African languages and today the various languages of the Americas. The Israelis (Khazars) spoke a Turkish language (Yiddish), which they still speak. The Israelites practised the religion of their forefathers as commanded by their God through Moses and written in their book, the Holy Bible. The Israelis practise a pagan philosophy called Judaism. The Israelites travelled by way of the Red Sea and the Jordan; while the Khazars travelled by way of the Caspian Sea and the Volga, and the Edomites by way of the Dead or Salt Sea and the Arabah. The Israelites came from Canaan through the lineage of Abraham, Isaac and Jacob; while the Khazars came from the Caucasus through Gomer, Togarmah and Khazar and the Edomites from Mount Seir through Abraham, Isaac and Esau or Edom. Finally, according to the Holy Bible, God Himself selected the Israelites and hated the Edomites (Malachi 1:1-5), while according to history, the Khazars were chosen by men.

THE ISRAELITES GOD'S ELECT
by Michael Hinds

There are many factors which distinguish the Israelites from other people. Their spiritual blessings come to mind first. But their dispersal, enslavement and constant oppression are equally as important. Without trying to rewrite the bible, we will highlight some of these distinguishing features, in order to gain a good understanding of these people whom God has selected for Himself. We shall also address the Israelites in light of biblical prophecy while drawing on historical facts, as well as current conditions, to demonstrate the manifestations of the prophecies.

ORIGINS

Now let us examine the origins of the Israelites. **Genesis 35:9-12** "And God appeared unto Jacob again, when he came out of Padanaram, and blessed him. And God said unto him, Thy name is Jacob; thy name shall not be called anymore Jacob, but Israel shall be thy name; and he called his name Israel. And God said unto him, I am God Almighty; be fruitful and multiply; a nation and a company of nations shall be of thee, and kings shall come out of thy loins; and the land which I gave Abraham and Isaac, to thee I will give it, and to thy seed after thee will I give the land." Here God selects the name for His people. When we refer to the children of Israel or Israelites, we speak of the descendants of Jacob or Israel. There were twelve sons as follows: Reuben, Simeon, Levi, Judah, Zebulun, Issachar, Dan, Gad, Naphtali, Joseph and Benjamin. Today, due to their dispersal and enslavement, it is next to impossible to determine from which tribe an Israelite originated. To be an Israelite is not a status symbol, but rather a symbol of obedience to God, a symbol of truth.

GOD'S PEOPLE IDENTIFIED

God is creator of all, but Father ONLY to the Israelites. **Jeremiah 31:9** states, "They shall come with weeping, and with supplications will I lead them: I will cause them to walk by the rivers of waters in a straight way, wherein they shall not stumble: FOR I AM A FATHER TO ISRAEL, and Ephraim is my first born." **Amos 3:1-2** says, "Hear this word that the Lord hath spoken against you. O CHILDREN OF ISRAEL, against the whole family which I brought up from the land of Egypt, saying, YOU ONLY HAVE I KNOWN OF ALL THE FAMILIES OF THE EARTH: Therefore I will punish you for all your iniquities." These scriptures are very clear. God says what He means and means what He says. We should not concern ourselves with why God selected the Israelites. The fact is He did, and being God Almighty, He is able to do whatsoever He wants. We should try to understand what the Israelites mean to God.

God has separated the Israelites making them different from all other people on the face of this earth. **Exodus 33:16** confirms this point; "For wherein shall it be known here that I and thy people have found grace in thy sight? Is it not in that thou goest with us? So shall we be separated, I and thy people, from all the people that are upon the face of the earth." This point is further reiterated in **Leviticus 20:26** "And ye shall be holy unto me: for I the Lord am holy, and have severed you from other people, that ye should be mine."

Deuteronomy 10:12-13 gives us some indication of the purpose or responsibility of an Israelite, "And now, Israel, what doth the Lord thy God require of thee, but to fear the Lord thy God, to walk in all his ways, and to love him, and to serve the Lord thy God with all thy heart and with all thy soul, To keep the commandments of the Lord, and his statutes which I command thee this day for thy good?" **I Peter 2:9** states, "But ye are a chosen generation, a royal priesthood, an holy nation, a peculiar people; that ye should shew forth the praises of Him who hath called you out of darkness into His marvellous light."

In **Romans 9:3-4** Paul writes, "For I could wish that myself were accursed from Christ for my brethren, my kinsmen according to the flesh: Who are ISRAELITES; to whom pertaineth the adoption, and the glory, and the covenants, and the giving of the law, and the service of God, and the promises."

Isaiah 43:10-12 says, "Ye are my WITNESSES, saith the Lord, and my servant whom I have chosen: that ye may know and believe me, and understand that I am he: before me there was no God formed, neither shall there be after me. I, even I, am the Lord; and besides me there is no saviour. I have declared, and have saved, and I have shewed, when there was no strange god among you: therefore ye are my witnesses, saith the Lord, that I am God." So the next time the so-called "Jehovah Witness", or any pagan Christian for that matter, knock on our door, we would know what to do. All these foregoing scriptures identify God's people, the ISRAELITES. They also indicate the responsibility of the Israelites and show the special relationship between them and their God. There should be no more confusion regarding this matter.

Furthermore, throughout the bible God is known as "The God of Israel", or "The God of Abraham, Isaac and Jacob." He is not the God of Christianity, or the God of Islam. They have their own gods. In addition, the God of Israel made a covenant (agreement) with the Israelites. **Exodus 34:27-28** states, "And the Lord said unto Moses, Write thou these words: for after the tenor of these words I have made a covenant with thee and with ISRAEL. And he was there with the Lord forty days and forty night; he did neither eat bread, nor drink water. And he wrote upon the tables the words or the covenant, the ten commandment." **Psalm 89:34-35** declares, "My covenant will I not break, nor alter the thing that is gone out of my lips. Once I have sworn by my holiness that I will not lie unto David." The covenant includes laws, statues and commandments and is **everlasting to all generations**. Therefore, Israelites today must be sure to adhere to the agreement made with their God. But who are the Israelites today?

THE MANIPULATORS

Much has been written and is being written about the small percentage of Israelites (Jews) who settled on the northern shores of the Mediterranean and Iberia. Estimates of approximately 20% of the total dispersal would be quite generous. The fact is, as we have proven before, many erroneously write of the Khazars or Eastern European Gentiles as Jews. They also erroneously equate the pagan doctrine of Judaism with the doctrine of the ancient Israelites. But we all have ourselves to blame for this travesty, because we willingly surrendered our ability to think for ourselves to others; that is, until now.

In addition, many of us chose to disregard what was written by the Israelites in the bible, in favour of the fiction and distortions spitefully concocted by the warped minds of Europe, especially those of the 1840's and 1850's. That was the period which gave birth to "RACISM" and "DARWINISM". Such were the tools of the disciples of Lucifer, which helped to sow the seeds of deceit and distrust among humanity. Thus humanity was cruelly divided, minds enslaved and a wedge driven between God and His people. Of course, all along a more sinister plot was being hatched. The plan was to replace God's chosen people with another. So effective were the tools of the manipulators, that had it not been for the God of the Israelites, the disciples of Lucifer would have been successful.

But it would appear as if Lucifer first deceived his own. It was only since 1492, a mere 500 years ago, that the same "brilliant" minds of Europe became fully satisfied that our planet was not flat. The book of Genesis, written by an Israelite, was available for over 2500 years. All that was required was to read it to gain some valuable insight regarding our universe.

Also, we must know that it was a German, **Johann Friedrich Blumenbach (1752-1840)** who first attempted to change the **THREE RACES** of humanity into five. He divided humanity by skin colour and acclaimed the Caucasian the original, **contrary to all existing facts**, especially the scriptures.

All this evil was spawned at the University of Gottingen, Germany in 1734. Gottingen became the breeding ground of racism, or more accurately, the theory of white supremacy. As a British/German effort, it was spearheaded by King George II of England. The British, steeped in the slave trade, badly needed justification for their wickedness. Johann Blumenbach was a product of this disease, which was deeply rooted in Christianity.

However, we shall concentrate on the majority of Israelites who were dispersed to Western Africa. We shall even prove that the greater part of the small Israelite settlements in Southern Europe, eventually fled to Western Africa to avoid persecution. We shall further demonstrate that the children of Israel are alive today in the lands of their captivity, the Americas, as prophesied in the bible. But before we address their dispersal, let us examine their sojourn in the land of Ham-Egypt.

THE HYKSOS OR SHEPHERD KINGS

Of all the nations of the ancient world (excluding the Israelites) the Egyptians left us the most detailed record of their history. For over 3000 years, all their important events, including a list of rulers, have been recorded in some form. However, there is a period of about 230 years in Egyptian history, for which there is little or no account. The Egyptologists are put to confusion. The period spans the XIIIth to XVIIth Dynasties, from approximately 1800 B.C. to 1570 B.C. For such a highly developed black people, with their very advanced civilization and meticulous track record, this is a mystery.

It was just prior to this period of missing records, when Egypt was at its weakest, that the Israelites arrived, around 1876 B.C. These Israelites, or Shepherd Kings would later form the XVth and XVIth Dynasties. The Egyptians called them "Rulers of a foreign country" and from their capital at Avaris in the delta, the Israelites ruled Egypt for over 200 years. The proud Egyptians used to look down upon the desert nomads and sheep herders. It was therefore, quite an embarrassment to admit to the world that these same "lowly" people subjugated them at the height of their civilization, and for such a long time. This factor would definitely play a role in the silent period of Egyptian history.

Of course many historians would want to challenge these facts. But before we start the debate, we should always consider the spiritual component. We must understand that the God of the Israelites gave the Egyptians their power, so He should have no problem taking that power away. As always, the proof is in the scriptures. Just prior to the Exodus of the Israelites, God manipulated the Egyptian Pharaoh. **Exodus 10:1-2** states, "And the Lord said unto Moses, Go in unto Pharaoh: for I have hardened his heart, and the heart of his servants, that I might shew these my signs before him: And that thou mayest tell in the ears of thy son, and of thy son's son what things I have wrought in Egypt, and my signs which I have done among them; that ye may know how that I am the Lord." Poor Pharaoh, he would have been only too happy to rid Egypt of the Israelites, yet just could not understand why he refused to let them go.

God also showed His power and control over Egypt in **Ezekiel 30:10-12** "Thus saith the Lord God; I will also make the multitude of Egypt to cease by the hand of Nebuchadnezzar, king of Babylon. He and his people with him, the terrible of the nations, shall be brought to destroy the land: and they shall draw their swords against Egypt, and fill the land with the slain. And I will make the rivers dry, and sell the land into the hand of the wicked: and I will make the land waste, and all that is therein, by the hand of strangers: I the Lord have spoken it." We could only imagine Pharaoh laughing at the threat of Ezekiel's prophecy. At that time the Babylonians and the Egyptians ruled the world. Here is some food for thought. Egypt had to be punished for 40 years by the God of Israel for their treatment of the Israelites prior to their Exodus. The God of Israel wanted to reward Nebuchadnezzar for his service in fighting against the king of Tyrus. Egypt was a Babylonia territory for forty years and Nebuchadnezzar died after only 43 years as king, at the height of his glory. He was the most powerful man on earth. But back to the Hyksos.

In **<u>Genesis 46:31-34</u>**, we can see why the Israelites were called Shepherd Kings; "And Joseph said unto his brethren, and unto his father's house, I will go up, and shew Pharaoh, and say unto him, My brethren, and my father's house, which were in the land of Canaan, unto me; And the men are SHEPHERDS, for their trade hath been to feed cattle; and have brought their flocks, and their herds, and all that they have. And it shall come to pass when Pharaoh shall call you, and shall say, What is your occupation? That ye shall say, Thy servants' trade hath been about cattle from our youth even until now, both we, and also our fathers: that ye may dwell in the land of Goshen; **for every shepherd is an abomination unto the Egyptians.**" Those of us who abide by truth, logic and common sense would have no problem reconciling these scriptures with the facts of history.

In the British Museum, the text of the Orbiney Papyrus relates a story entitled "The Tale of Two Brothers." This document is very similar in substance to the biblical story detailing Joseph's refusal to lie with Potiphar's wife. The date of the Orbiney Papyrus anyhow, is about the time of the 19th Dynasty, shortly after the Exodus.

Furthermore, **<u>Genesis 41:42</u>** gives us an exact account of Egyptian protocol for the induction of a Governor. "And Pharaoh took of his ring from his hand, and put it upon Joseph's hand and arrayed him in vestures of fine linen, and put a gold chain about his neck." This ceremony is clearly depicted on Egyptian wall paintings and sculptures. The ring or seal of the Pharaoh is similar symbolically to the Seal of the President of the United States.

In the British Museum is the "Papyrus Sallier I". It details communication between King Apophis of Avaris and the Egyptian Prince Sekeneure of Thebes. Apophis was the longest reigning Israelite king of sixty-one years. All Israelites ruled from Avaris (Ramses) in the land of Goshen.

<u>Genesis 50:2-3</u> clearly indicates the power and respect the Israelites commanded in Egypt. "And Joseph commanded his servants the physicians to embalm his father: and he embalmed Israel. And forty days were fulfilled for him; for so are fulfilled the days of those which are embalmed: and the Egyptians mourned for him threescore and ten days."

Genesis 50:7 states, "And Joseph went up to bury his father: and with him went up all the servants of Pharaoh, the elders of his house, and all the elders of the land of Egypt." Thus Jacob was given a "state funeral", a courtesy usually reserved for heads-of-state.

"Now there arose up a new king over Egypt, which knew not Joseph. And he said unto his people, Behold, the people of the children of Israel are more and mightier than we: Come on, let us deal wisely with them; lest they multiply, and it come to pass, that, when there falleth out any war, they join also unto our enemies, and fight against us, and so get them up out of the land." (**Exodus 1:8-10**). With this statement the period of the Israelite oppression began.

EXODUS

After four hundred and thirty years in the land of Ham, the Israelites left Egypt led by Moses under the direction of their God, the God of Abraham, Isaac and Jacob.

Many historians have dated the Exodus to correspond with Rameses II, around 1224 B.C. When this is measured against the standard of truth, the holy bible, it is found wanting. To avoid this conflict they question the accuracy of the bible. Let us examine the facts carefully.

1. The death of Solomon is fairly accurately placed around 930 B.C.

2. **I Kings 11:42** states that Solomon reigned for 40 years.

3. **I Kings 6:1** states that Solomon started building the temple during the fourth year of his reign (966 B.C.) and 480 years after the Exodus. Could this duration of 480 years represent 40 years for each tribe; i.e. 12x40=480?

4. **Exodus 12:40** states that the Israelites spent 430 years in Egypt. Therefore, 966+480=1446 B.C. (Exodus) +430 = 1876 B.C. (Arrival in Egypt).
This would place the Exodus at the end of the reign of Thutmose III (1486-1446).

Now let us look at the facts against a "Rameses II Exodus." **Genesis 47:11** states that the Israelites settled in **the land of Rameses**, while **Exodus 1:11** states that they built Pithom and Rameses. Both references to Rameses were made most likely after the Exodus, while the scriptures were being written. At such a time the name Rameses would have been more relevant since that Pharaoh started to rule around 1290 B.C. There is therefore no argument for a contradiction of scripture. Also, Pharaoh Merneptah invaded Canaan during the fifth year of his rule (1219 B.C.). A record of his exploits included the mention of Israel by name. This proves that the Israelites were already in the land of Canaan. Therefore, it would be next to impossible for the Israelites to exit Egypt around 1224 B.C., spend forty years in the wilderness and settle into Canaan in time to do battle with Merneptah.

This brings to a close the "silent period" of Egyptian history, the period of the Hyksos or Israelites, between the XIIIth and XVIIIth Dynasties. Now many a Christian preacher, so-called historians and others have stated that the Israelites have been enslaved in Egypt for 400 years. We have, therefore, proven them to be all wrong. But this was not the only error they made. Actually it was a lie, not an error, since it was done presumptuously as part of another motive. Let us move now to North Eastern Africa to the land of Canaan. Please note there is no such place as "the Middle East", just like there is no "Third World" or no "World War". These are "terms of convenience" for some, part of that "other motive".

THE PHOENICIAN CONNECTION

Throughout their history the Israelites and the Phoenicians were so close that many historians and authors have referred to both nationalities as being Semitic. Let us read **Genesis 10:6** in order to get the truth. "And the sons of Ham; Cush, and Mizraim, and Phut, and Canaan." Next **Genesis 10:19** "And the border of the Canaanites was from Sidon, as thou comest to Gerar, unto Gaza; as thou goest unto Sodom and Gomorrah..." Phoenician is just another name for Sidonian.

Thus the Phoenicians were Hamitic, just like the Ethiopians, Egyptians, Libyans and the Canaanites, and not Semitic.

Another important point to note is that the Hamites were all BLACK, or as the Portuguese would later refer to them, along with the Jews (Israelites), "negro". We are still to find a place or country on our planet called "Negro", yet there are so many "Negroes". Where did they all come from? Again truth, logic and common sense would dictate that "negro" means "black", just like "moor" and has nothing to do with nationality. The land (country) derived its name from the people who lived therein.

Sidon was the first born of Canaan. The co-operation between the Phoenicians and the Israelites goes back to the days of the construction of the Temple at Jerusalem by King Solomon. As we read **I Kings 5:1-2**, many Phoenicians were employed by Solomon; "And Hiram king of Tyre sent his servants unto Solomon; for he had heard that they had anointed him king in the room of his father: for Hiram was ever a lover of David. And Solomon sent to Hiram, saying," **Verse 6** "Now therefore command thou that they hew me cedar trees out of Lebanon; and my servants shall be with thy servants: and unto thee will I give hire for thy servants according to all that thou shalt appoint: for thou knowest that there is not among us any that can skill to hew timber like unto the Sidonians."

The Phoenicians also transported gold from Ophir to Israel for King Solomon. **I Kings 9:27-28** states, "And Hiram sent in the navy his servants, shipmen that had knowledge of the sea, with the servants of Solomon. And they came to Ophir, and fetched from thence gold, four hundred and twenty talents, and brought it to king Solomon." We should understand that Phoenicia, Sidon, Tyre or Tyrus and Lebanon are all the same. Later we shall examine the location of Ophir.

The Phoenicians were excellent mariners, while the Israelites were good business people. This combination was ideal for colonization; so the Phoenicians established the colonies while the Israelites developed the commerce. Carthage, (Tunis) on the north coast of Africa was one such operation. It grew from a town around 826 B.C. (almost 300 years before the founding of Rome by the Etruscans) to an Empire controlling both sides of the Mediterranean Sea, west of Egypt on the south and Greece on the north. It would be in these Mediterranean areas that the dispersed Israelites would later settle. Again according to truth, logic and common sense, it would be the children of Ham, who fled Palestine when Joshua led the Israelites into the Promised Land, that settled on the northern shores of Africa. At Tigisis, in Numidia (Algeria) a land mark column with a Phoenician-type script state, "We are they who fled from before the face of Joshua, the robber, the son of Nun." Now we can understand why the Phoenicians were so successful in this region, their relatives settled there earlier.

When we understand that Canaan was cursed by Noah for his wickedness and sentenced to a life of servitude, we can begin to appreciate the relationship between the Israelites and the Canaanites. **Genesis 9:24-26** says "And Noah awoke from his wine, and knew what his younger son had done unto him. And he said, Cursed be Canaan; a servant of servants shall he be unto his brethren. And he said, Blessed be the Lord God of Shem; and Canaan shall be his servant." Now we shall explore this service even further.

About 600 B.C., at the request of Pharaoh Necho II, the Phoenicians circumnavigated the African continent. Then in 500 B.C., Hanno, the great Carthaginian explorer, sailed out into the Atlantic and along the western coast of Africa to the region of the Cameroon. Later, the Greek historian Herodotus would write concerning the trade between Carthage and West Africa. From the time of King Solomon there were Carthaginian colonies along the western coast of Africa. **I Kings 10:22** says, "For the king had at sea a navy of Tharshish with the navy of Hiram: once in three years came the navy of Tharshish, bringing gold, and silver, ivory, and apes, and peacocks." Tharshish was a silver producing Phoenician / Carthaginian colony of southern Iberia (Spain). Gold (Gold Coast), ivory (Ivory Coast) and apes are all found in abundance in West Africa. The peacock is a tropical bird which would thrive best in the jungle of West Africa.

Let us now examine further, the name "Ophir" from a cultural perspective, remembering that the land derived its name from the people who lived therein. "ophir" in the ancient Hebrew language meant "of or relating to the serpent." In the Greek language "ophis" means serpent. Today we have "ophiolatry", which is "serpent-worship." From the time of Genesis the serpent has been identified as Lucifer. Also, during the time of the Babylonians, serpent-worship along with fire-worship was practised simultaneously. (We all should know by now that a dragon exhales fire!) Every Pharaoh wore the head of the serpent on his crown. The Canaanites also engaged in serpent- and/or fire-worship and they passed it on to the Phoenicians, Israelites and Carthaginians. Ophir was originally a Phoenician/Carthaginian colony located in western Africa.

Not only is the land being prepared, but the culture as well. Unknowingly the Israelites are being introduced to the regions that would play a big role in their future lives, i.e. their re-settlement in Northern and finally Western Africa.

Let us continue to look briefly at the cultural aspect. Ophiolatry or serpent-worship is highly spiritual and all these black people are extremely spiritual, even today. This brings us to "oub" (Egyptian), "ob" (Hebrew), "aub" (Canaanite) "obi" (Ashanti), or "obeah" (West Indian). ("ob-, oub-, aub- and eph-" are variations of "oph"). Thus the Egyptian serpent-god was "Ob" or "Oub." In the ancient Hebrew language "Ob" meant "a necromancer, a wizard, magician or sorcerer." The supreme ruler of Benin (Nigeria) was called "Oba or Obba." Voodoo, or ancestral worship is only another version of serpent worship.

THE DISPERSAL OF THE ISRAELITES

The facts of history determines what major factors led to the dispersal of the Israelites from the Promised Land. The Israelites were disobedient towards their God and worshipped other gods. For this they had to be punished. Many people still do not believe in the word of God and consider the Holy Scriptures to be a collection of fairy tales. The choice is ours!

But at least we should try to understand what happened to the Israelites and see if there is anything we could learn from their mistakes.

In **Leviticus 26:33** God warned through Moses, "And I will scatter you among the heathen, and will draw out a sword after you: and your land shall be desolate, and your cities waste." Again God warned through Moses in **Deuteronomy 28:49-50** "The Lord shall bring a nation against thee from far, from the end of the earth, as swift as the eagle flieth; a nation whose tongue thou shalt not understand; A nation of fierce countenance, which shall not regard the person of the old, nor shew favour to the young:" **Verse 52** states, " And he shall besiege thee in all thy gates, until thy high and fenced walls come down, wherein thou trustedst, throughout all thy land: and he shall besiege thee in all thy gates throughout all thy land, which the Lord thy God hath given thee." Let us never forget these scriptures, because these warnings were given by Moses before the Israelites entered the Promised Land. Now let us see what happened!

Within a year after the death of Solomon in 930 B.C., the kingdom of the Israelites was divided into Israel to the north and Judea to the south. This division was caused by internal strife which continued periodically for the next one hundred years. God sent Isaiah with another warning saying,(**Isaiah 10:5-6**) "O Assyrian, the rod of mine anger, and the staff in their hand is mine indignation. I will send him against an hypocritical nation, and against the people of my wrath will I give him a charge, to take the spoil, and to take the prey, and to tread them down like the mire of the streets."

In 722 B.C. the Assyrian king Sargon II captured Samaria, the capital of Israel. He deported some 30,000 Israelites to Babylon.

However, there was no change in Judea, so God sent Jeremiah saying, (**Jeremiah 20:4-5**) "For thus saith the Lord, Behold, I will make thee a terror to thyself, and to all thy friends: and they shall fall by the sword of their enemies, and thine eyes shall behold it: and I will give all Judah into the hand of the king of Babylon, and he shall carry them captive into Babylon, and shall slay them with the sword. Moreover I will deliver all the strength of this city, and all the labours thereof, and all the precious thing thereof, and all the treasures of the kings of Judah will I give into the hand of their enemies, which shall spoil them, and take them, and carry them to Babylon."

In 597 B.C. the Babylonian king Nebuchadnezzar II invaded Judea. After waging a three year war, he captured Jerusalem and took approximately 20,000 of it chief citizens back to Babylon. But Judea refused to be submissive.

In 586 B.C. Nebuchadnezzar II returned again to Jerusalem. This time he pillaged the city and destroyed the temple, taking the majority of the population captive to Babylon. Even after the return from captivity the Israelites refused to change their ways. Of course Jeremiah had already delivered the warning from God saying, (**Jeremiah 4:6-7**) "Set up the standard toward Zion: retire, stay not: for I will bring evil from the north, and a great destruction. The lion is come up from his thicket, and the destroyer of the Gentiles is on his way; he is gone forth from his place to make thy land desolate; and thy cities shall be laid waste, without an inhabitant."

Then came the Greeks in 168 B.C., led by the Selucid king Antiochus IV or Ephiphanes. He tried to "Helenize" the Israelites by enforcing pagan worship of idols. Antiochus captured Jerusalem, murdering thousands of Israelites in the process. He plundered and defiled the Temple, installing idols and sacrificing swine's flesh upon the altar. In addition, Antiochus prohibited the observance of the Sabbath and the circumcision of male infants. But the Israelites led by the Maccabees, fought a twenty-three year war (167-144B.C.) against the Greeks in order to defend their honour. There arose Mattathias, a Levite, who refused to be subjected to such barbaric Gentile customs. Together with his five sons (Maccabees) he fought and defeated the Greek pagans, restoring the holiness of the Temple by 164 B.C. and the full independence of Judea by 143 B.C.

Weakened again by internal strife, Judea was invaded by Pompey in 63 B.C. and Roman rule commenced. From this point on the lights of the Israelites in Palestine gradually dimmed. The Roman General Titus put the last nail in the coffin, when in 70 A.D., after a four year seize of Jerusalem, he destroyed the Temple. Titus acted like a mad man as he raped and massacred at will. Those who survived were sold as slaves.

These were the major factors which caused the Israelites to flee the Promised Land and become refugees among the heathens of the world. By the year 135 A.D. practically all Israelites were dispersed from Palestine NEVER to see that land again. But where did they all go?

FROM PALESTINE TO WESTERN SUDAN

Throughout all the turmoil occurring in and around Palestine, the Israelites sought a safe haven in many countries. Some returned to Babylon; others settled in Asia (Turkey) and Cyprus; a few went to Greece when they ruled in Judea; some to Rome and Roman colonies both as free men and slaves; yet others fled as far as India. Of course we all know of the Falashas or Beta Israel and the Israelites of Yemen. But we shall concentrate on the greater numbers who fled to West Africa or Western Sudan. They came to West Africa by three main routes: 1) from the Nile region west between the corridor of the Sahara and the tropical forest; 2) from Northern Africa across the Sahara; and 3) from Iberia (Spain/Portugal) by sea and land. It was only in West Africa that the tribes of Israel found some peace with prosperity at least until the Muslims arrived. But by then it was too late; they had forgotten how to worship their God. Let us examine the first and second routes taken to West Africa.

FROM THE NILE TO THE NIGER

Israelites have been seeking refuge in Egypt from as early as 586 B.C. Many settled in the delta region before travelling up the Nile to Elephantine Island at the First Cataract. When Cambyses conquered Egypt in 525 B.C., he found a temple at Elephantine dedicated to the God of Israel. Papyri documents written in Aramaic have been found at Elephantine dating back to 500 B.C. Later, at Alexandria, the Israelites accounted for a sizable portion of the population. They were specially favoured under the Ptolemies and enjoyed religious freedom and local self rule. It was at Alexandria under Ptolemy II (Philadelphus), around 250 B.C. that seventy two Israelites translated the Old Testament scriptures into Greek. When these scriptures were first revealed to King Ptolemy II by the Israelites, he bowed seven times before them while thanking them and their God.

After leaving Egypt, as if by fate, some Israelites pushed further south into the heart of Africa beyond Khartum in the Sudan. Still following the course of the Nile, at Kordofan along the White Nile, they turned westwards, although a few went on to settle in Uganda. Others joined from Yemen and Arabia as they trekked by way of Darfur and Wadai to Lake Chad. From Chad they were free to settle among any of the many communities which extended westward to the Atlantic.

FROM NORTH AFRICA
TO THE NIGER

Not all the Israelites who fled to Africa settled in Egypt. Cyrenaica or Pentapolis in Libya which became an Egyptian province under Ptolemy I (Soter) in 320 B.C., was also a predominantly Israelite settlement. It enjoyed local self government and was headed by a Levite. **Matthew 27:32** states, "And as they came out, they found a man of Cyrene, Simon by name: him they compelled to bear his cross." Many Christian preachers are quick to point to the blackness of Simon, and correctly so, obviously because he was forced to do the dirty work for Jesus. But what they would never understand is that to an Israelite it is always an honour and a privilege to serve the brethren. Then how would they explain a "white" Jesus? Had it not been for "the kiss of death" from Judas, the Roman soldiers could not even identify Jesus from his brethren. Also, **Acts chapter two** indicates that there were men from Egypt and Cyrene who received the Holy Spirit on the day of Pentecost. Later, the Israelites of Cyrenaica would suffer severely at the hand of the Roman pagan Emperors.

Carthage, with its hinterland of Numidia and Mauretania (Algeria/Morocco), also played a very important role in the lives of the Israelites. The Israelite population was small compared to other regions, probably because most Carthaginians worshipped Baal. However, the Israelites would have a tremendous impact on the shaping of Christianity, although the very existence of Christianity today would testify to their failure. The religious leadership originated with the peasants of Numidia, who referred to themselves as **Nazarenes** and not Christians. Of course all Nazarenes, like Jesus, were Israelites. The Nazarenes were in constant conflict with the pagan Romans, as they showed loyalty to the Roman Emperor, but steadfastly refused to worship him. For this they suffered severe persecution by the Romans. There were several black leaders, whose education in the doctrine of the Nazarenes helped to sow the seeds of Western civilization before the arrival of the European "Vandals" in 430 A.D.

Tertullian 160-225 A.D., was constantly at odds with the pagan Romans. The Christians called him the first great "theologian" and credited him with the introduction of Latin to their rituals. Cyprian 205-258) A.D. became Bishop of Carthage in 248. He was head of the Council of African Bishops, which was the most powerful religious body in existence. Later the Roman Papacy would become dominant, a position which they still maintain to this day. Cyprian strongly opposed Roman Emperor-worship and was beheaded by the Romans on September 14, 258 for his opposition.

Donatus of Casae Nigrae, Bishop of Carthage from 313-355 A.D., was head of the Council of African Bishops and leader of the Donatist Movement. An excellent orator and administrator whose sweeping religious reforms made him the biggest enemy of the Roman Christians and Emperor. Regarded as a prophet by his people, he not only followed the teachings of the Old Testament, but wanted to establish a kingdom similar to that of ancient Israel in the time of Solomon. He also declared the independence of the Council of African Bishops from the Papacy. For forty years he was a thorn in the side of the Romans and despite severe persecution from Rome the Donatist Movement survived for 300 years in

North Africa until the Islamic invasion. It was the Council of the African Bishops in 397 A.D., that selected, approved and fixed the twenty-seven books of the New Testament. The foresight of Donatus in teaching against the corruption of the pagan Christians is greatly appreciated today.

From the time of Roman Emperor Nero (54-68 A.D.), Jews (Israelites) were viciously persecuted. One of the most famous Israelites, Paul, was murdered by this mad man in 64 or 67 A.D. There were many laws enacted against the Israelites which denied them justice religiously, politically, economically, socially, etc. Any revolt against such treatment, and there were many, very often resulted in death. Such treatment occurred all over the Roman Empire. Many Israelites fled the northern lands of the Mediterranean (Rome, Greece, Asia, etc.) for the secured shores of Northern Africa. But this would only be temporary, since Roman jurisdiction extended to Northern Africa. It was beyond the Great Desert, the Sahara, where they found solace.

Even before the destruction of the Temple by Titus, there were trade routes across the Sahara, between North Africa and West Africa. These same routes would be used as life savers, when persecution from the Romans and other Europeans became unbearable. Wave after wave of Israelites fled the northern Mediterranean and Asia, as well as Northern Africa, for the Sahara Desert. It proved to be a welcomed barrier and the Israelite settlements of Western Africa, a sanctuary. Now we can appreciate the thought behind the geographical conditions that produced the desert.

From Cyrenaica and Leptis Magna Israelites met at Fezzan. Some went via Ghat, where they met the brethren from Carthage, and thence on to Timbuctu and Gao. Others went via the region of Air to Hausa; while some travelled to the salt producing town of Bilma linking up at Kanem-Bornu, around Lake Chad, with the brethren heading west from the Nile. From Carthage, Numidia and Mauretania they met at Tuat and thence on to Timbuctu and Jenne, via the salt producing towns of Taghaza and Taoderni.

WEST AFRICAN
ISRAELITE EMPIRES

With natural resources of gold, iron, ivory, the Niger, Senegal and Volta rivers, plus fertile soil and salt mines, the Kingdom of Ghana was well established by 200 A.D. or even earlier. The kingdom derived its name from the title of the Israelite king which was "Ghana". But another title was "Kaya Magan." This was derived from "Kay Mag" which means "one who is great." We are all familiar with the "Magen David", meaning "King David's Shield." However, due to sound political and economic skills, plus geographic isolation, Ghana prospered and rapidly grew into an Empire by the fifth century. By 790 A.D., there were already forty-four Israelite kings on record. Known throughout the world as the "Land of Gold", Ghana was one of the wealthiest Empires of its era. Its educational system was second only to the Egyptian, predating that of the Europeans by almost one thousand years. The main centre of learning was the University of Sankore at Timbuctu.

In 1076, a Muslim sect known as the ALMORAVIDS, invaded Ghana causing devastating consequences. They ravaged and plundered, then imposed heavy taxes, while forcing the Israelites to convert to Islam. Since the Muslims controlled the external commercial routes, many Israelites adopted Islam in the late tenth and eleventh centuries; but only as a matter of expediency. While Islam became the Imperial Cult and the philosophy of the state elite and traders, the rural population maintained their Israelite customs.

Ghana set the pattern for successive West African Israelite Empires. Both Mali and Songhai became more prosperous in turn. The Israelite king Sundiata built the Mali Kingdom from the ruins of Ghana and in 1238 founded the Mali Empire. The popular Israelite explorer Mansa Musa (converted to Islam) ruled from 1307-1332. Due to his leadership, the wealth, grandeur and dignity of Mali was recognized world-wide.

Songhai replace Mali in 1488 under Sunni Ali, another Islamic convert, who merely paid lip service to the cult. On the other hand, Askia Mohammed I took full advantage of the

Islamic cult to achieve his political objectives. He greatly expanded and improved the educational, political and economic systems, while ruling Songhai from 1493-1528. In 1591 another Islamic invasion brought an end to the Songhai Empire.

Western African splendour was known by the Romans since 19 B.C. when Septimus Flaccus visited the region. Later Seutonis Paulinus reached the Niger in 50 A.D., and Julius Maternus even later. Therefore, at the time of Paul, that famous Israelite, the Romans were well aware of the identity and appearance of the Israelites. **Acts 13:1** states, "Now there were in the church that was at Antioch certain prophets and teachers; as Barnabas, and Simeon that was called Niger, and Lucius of Cyrene, and Manaen, which had been brought up with Herod the tetrarch, and Saul." Just as Egyptians were affiliated with the Nile and the Europeans with the Caucasus Mountains, hence the Jews were identified with the Niger.

It should come as no surprise then, that the king of Alban (Scotland) from 962-967 A.D. would be known as "Niger," "Dubh," or "The Black." Another one of his titles was the "Cinaed," or "Kinat." This later became "Kenneth," then "Kennettie," then "Kennedy." So now we know that "Kennedy" was not an original surname, but simply referred to the black king of Scotland. Going back to the "Magen David," however, it is interesting to note that the same king of Scotland was called the "Maga Dubh," meaning the "Black King." From this we got "Mac Duff," meaning "the son of the Black" and "Dubh Gall," which led to "Douglas," meaning "black stranger." Now where did "Dublin" come from?

THE ISLAMIC INVASION

"And the angel of the Lord said unto her, Behold, thou art with child, and shalt bear a son, and shalt call his name Ishmael; because the Lord hath heard thy affliction. And he will be a wild man; his hand will be against every man, and every man's hand against him; and he shall dwell in the presence of all his brethren." **Genesis 16:11-12**.

By way of this prophecy, God has introduced a key player who will figure prominently in the destiny of His people. As we have already noticed, the role of Ishmael, the father of the Ishmaelites or Muslims, will be one of destruction and warfare; therefore proving the accuracy of the scriptures. Ishmael then, must play the role of the enemy of God, by being the enemy of God's children, the Israelites; and how well he has played it. Woe unto him!

Most black people of the Americas (Israelites) are taught only of the evils of the white man or European, but very little or nothing is ever mentioned concerning the atrocities of the BLACK MUSLIMS or ARABS towards the Israelites.

The point is that we must blame both the Gentile and the Ishmaelite, or none at all. Furthermore, it should be now quite evident that it is not a matter of colour, since both the Ishmaelite and the Israelite were black with woolly hair. In other words, the role of colour is a minor one. In fact, the issue of colour is used to mask a more sinister plot. Let us see what facts are available to illustrate the attitude of the Ishmaelite towards the Israelite.

In 622 A.D., Muhammed's own people, the Quraish tribe, threatened to kill him. The Israelites offered him a sanctuary at Yathrib or Medina. Two years later Muhammed would show his appreciation, by attacking and murdering hundreds of Israelite men and selling their women and children into slavery. All this Muhammed did because the "People of the Book" refused to be converted to Islam and laughed at him when he tried to explain their scriptures, claiming to be the promised Messiah.

In 624 A.D. the Muslims were in control of Cyrenaica, causing many Israelites to flee across the Sahara for their safety, since they refused to convert to Islam. But some Israelites decided to fight back.

In 682 A.D. the Israelite General Kuseila led his brethren of Mauretania and Numidia to victory over Ogbar-ben-Nafi. the Muslim Governor of Ifrigiah. Kuseila became king of Mauretania until 688 A.D. when he was killed in battle with the Muslims. But his relative Dahia-al-Kahina took up the challenge, driving the Muslims into Tripolitania. Queen Kahina ruled until 705 A.D. when she died in battle. This

Israelite heroine, who was also a Priestess, will always be remembered for her wisdom, courage and beauty. Many of her brethren fled south across the desert, refusing to convert to Islam. But one of her Generals did convert.

By 708 A.D. all North Africa was under Muslim control. The Israelite General Tarik-ibn-Ziad was converted to Islam and was made Governor of Tangier. In 711 A.D., as Governor of Mauretania, Tarik invaded Spain, with an army of seven thousand Israelites and other Africans, plus three hundred Ishmaelites or Muslims, defeating King Roderic in the process.

In 712 A.D. along came Musa-ibn-Nusayr with ten thousand Muslims, and eight thousand Israelites and other Africans. He chastised Tarik for being too aggressive, probably because of jealousy and jailed him. But the Caliphate freed Tarik and recalled Musa. Tarik then continued his conquest to the Pyrenees.

THE ORIGINS
OF WESTERN EUROPEAN
CIVILIZATION

It should be quite evident by now that the twelve tribes of Israel represent the "soul" of the world; that their God, the God of Truth, is the "Spirit" of the world and the rest of humanity, the "body". Therefore, it is only with the unity of these three principals that the best is achieved. We know from history, despite the lies of many, that the Gentile or European has not achieved anything on his own. The Egyptians taught the Greeks and the Babylonians (Etruscans) taught the Romans. Many again have tried unsuccessfully to put a white face on the ancient Egyptians and Babylonians. But here again we have the European being taught and for whatever it is worth, "black" teaching "white". We might as well get use to it because it will happen again very soon. So what is the big deal?

With the arrival of the Israelites in Iberia, Western Europe commenced its education, especially Germany and England. The Israelites first came with the Phoenicians, then with the

Romans after the destruction of their temple. Now under Tarik, who converted to Islam, the Israelites became world leaders in science, astronomy, mathematics, finance, philosophy, literature, religion, medicine and geography. All this exciting activity occurred in Spain, which became the most educationally advanced country in the world between 900 and 1300 A.D. Spain was the centre of European cultural activity and was very prosperous. All the nations of Europe came to Spain to drink from the fountain of knowledge, predominantly Israelite knowledge. Later many Europeans would falsely lay claim as the originators of this knowledge, some even perverting it for evil purposes. But we should always ask ourselves how come the European explorers originated from Iberia, specifically Portugal; and European science originated in the west. Let us now look at some of the outstanding contributions made by Israelites to the civilization of the Europeans.

ISAAC ALFASI (1013-1103). Born in Algeria (Numidia), lived in Fez (Morocco), fled to Cordova, Spain in 1088. He transferred the Babylonian Talmud to Lucena, Spain where he established the centre of Talmudic learning and dedicated the rest of his life to teaching. He became the leading Talmudic scholar and helped to lay the foundations of European civilization.

ABRAHAM ben SAMUEL ABULAFIA (1240-1292), Saragossa, Spain. He became the leading scholar in the development of what is today known as the "Kabbalah". This is a philosophy of esoteric mysticism based on theoretical or speculative ideas, with an attempt to unlock the mysteries of the bible. The main text of "Kabbalism" was the "Zohar" or "Book of Splendor", written by MOSES de LEON (1250-1305). Due mainly to these two Israelites Spain became the leading centre for mysticism. Later ABRAHAM ibn LATIF (1220-1290), would combine "Kabbalism" with mathematics, philosophy and natural science to help form the basis of European scientific knowledge. Unfortunately, many Europeans, lacking in spiritual understanding, separated the teachings of the "Kabbalah" from the bible and perverted the knowledge given by the Israelites. Many used it to gain power and foolishly tried to decipher the nature of God.

LEVI ben GERSHON (1288-1344), mathematician, astronomer and philosopher. He invented the QUADRANT, an instrument for taking angular measurements in navigation, astronomy and surveying. It was also know as "Jacob's Ladder" and was used by Christopher Columbus, Vasco da Gama and Ferdinand Magellan. Today it is called a sextant and no ship captain would ever leave port without one. Gershon also wrote extensively on trigonometry and paved the way for students like Johann Muller of Nuremberg, who Europeans presumptuously called "the father of trigonometry".

HASDAI CRESCAS (1340-1410), Barcelona, Spain; High Priest of Aragon and philosopher. His work of 1397, "A Refutation of the Principles of the Christians", conclusively proved the falsehood of Christianity and especially the concept of the "Trinity". His other major work of 1410, "The Light of the Lord", refuted the philosophy of Aristotle regarding matter, space and time. This shook up the entire European philosophical foundation, as Crescas demonstrated the infinity of space and time, based on his biblical knowledge. Thus, this Israelite was able to lay the foundation for Galileo, Descartes, Newton, Kant and Spinoza.

ABRAHAM ZACUTO (1450-1510), astronomer and assistant to King John II of Portugal. He produced the astronomical tables and charts used by both Christopher Columbus and Vasco de Gama. He taught astronomy at the universities of Salamanca and Saragossa and helped to pave the way for early European science.

These are some of the many Israelites who dominated the "Golden Age of Spain", from 900 to 1300 and helped to sow the seeds of civilization in Western Europe. Why are these facts not taught in our history classes at school?

FROM IBERIA TO WEST AFRICA

In 1478, under King Ferdinand and Queen Isabella, the Spanish Inquisition was established. The "Inquisitor-General" was Tomas de Torquemada, who was a Christian priest. The Inquisition was a secret institution established to protect and promote the pagan philosophy of Christianity, by expelling, forcibly converting, or murdering those who were not Christians. It acted as both police, prosecutor, and judge, with all its decisions being final. Many Israelites had their property confiscated, while others were burnt alive or tortured. Approximately 50,000 Israelites converted to Christianity.

On March 31, 1492, Ferdinand and Isabella issued a decree expelling all Jews (Israelites) from Spain. By August 2, 1492 some 120,000 Israelites would find temporary settlement in Portugal after paying a head tax of one ducat each, plus surrendering one quarter of their possessions. Many others fled to northern Africa, only to be rejected by the dominant Muslim society. Fortunately there were a few Israelite communities to receive them, yet most perished.

But the Portuguese had their own Inquisition. From since 1484 King Joao (or John) II (1481-1495) continued to ship Israelites who rejected Christianity to the island of San Thome or St. Thomas, off the coast of West Africa. Finally, in 1496 King Manoel issued his decree expelling all Israelites from Portugal. Those who were fortunate fled to North Africa, others perished or were sold into slavery.

This new influx of Israelites from Iberia increased the trek to Western Africa. Many came by way of the Atlas Mountains across the Western Sahara to West Africa, where they joined others from before. Gradually they would lose much of their original culture, but still clung to many biblical customs.

CONCLUSION

We have all been taught not to deal with "religion", just leave it to the "church". As we have seen religion is the most important element of life, especially for the Blackman of the Americas. This is the way it was from the beginning, in the Garden of Eden and nothing has changed. Even among the European Gentiles, their so-called religion drives all their activity. Few will ever understand that we live in the era of the **Christian Empire**, driven by a Christian culture. This culture has taught us of an ungodly African savage, who would have to be enslaved to be civilized and Christianized or "saved".

We should then ask ourselves why were the first Christian missionaries (Dominicans), who left Portugal for West Africa required to have a knowledge of Aramaic. We should know that Aramaic was the language spoken by Jesus the Christ and his Israelite brethren. Then we should question the fact that the slaves were not freed immediately after being "saved". In fact the chains of mental slavery are proving more effective today than the yokes our ancestors wore around their necks.

Now that we have started to think, figure this out:- why would the Kaffir, Ibo, Koromantyn, Grebo, Maribuck, Mavumba, Akra, Yoruba, Kongo, Ashanti, just to name a few, engage in ancient Israelite rituals? Such rituals included circumcision, the division of their tribes into twelve; blood sprinkling upon their altars and door-posts; marrying of their brother's wife after death; separation and purification after child birth; uncleanliness during menstruation and new moon celebrations. Many Christians were also surprised to learn that these so-called ungodly savages awaited a Messiah, long before the arrival of the first European Gentiles.

In 1874, the "Illustrated London News", on page 28, depicted a drawing of the Ashanti High Priest or Osene. He was seated on a raft while crossing the Prah river and accompanied by his assistants and two British soldiers. On his chest he wore a golden breastplate with twelve divisions, (ref. **Exodus 39**). On his head-dress was a gold disc with the inscription, "Holiness to the Lord", in his language. Among the Ashanti the priesthood is hereditary to a specific family. Such a family has little or no possessions, is exempt from all taxes, supplied with food and advises the king. Compare with the Levities of ancient Israel. Also the God of the Ashanti is Yame or Nyame; compare with Yahweh.

The Falasha used to call Western Sudan "the Land of the Hebrews". The Muslims used to refer to it as "Yahoodee" meaning "the Tribes of Israel". The Muslims were the first to inform the Portuguese of "the People of the Book, living in great numbers to the south of the desert - a race cursed of God and predestines as slaves." Then the stage was set for the greatest evil ever perpetrated against humanity - **the trading of some fifty million Israelites between black Muslims and white Christians.**

Of course the Muslims were correct in their statement to the Portuguese. In **<u>Genesis 15:13</u>**, the God of the Israelites spoke the prophecy Himself: "And He said unto Abram, Know of a surety that thy seed shall be a stranger in a land that is not theirs, and shall serve them; and they shall afflict them four hundred year." Moses also added his prophecy in **<u>Deuteronomy 28:68</u>** "And the Lord shall bring thee into Egypt again with ships, by the way whereof I spake unto thee, Thou shalt see it no more again: and there ye shall be sold unto your enemies for bondmen and bondwomen, and no man shall buy you." Note that Egypt is symbolic for a land of oppression as used in **Hosea chapters 8-9**.

Now that the four hundred years are drawing to a close, let us examine the mystery of the "Negro Spirituals." Many have referred to these songs as American Folksongs. There is nothing American about these songs, but rather everything clearly indicates an Israelite lamentation. The spirit of the Twelve Tribes of Israel crying out to their God, the God of Abraham, Isaac and Jacob, crying for mercy and salvation. The culture is not even African, but an Israelite spiritual experience - the very same foundation of Moses, Joshua, David, Solomon, and Jesus the Christ.

It is extremely important to note that nothing was sung about the Nile, Sphinx, Pyramids, Saraha, Niger, Congo, "Good Friday," "Easter," or even "Christmas". Instead, the slaves sang about everything in the scriptures from Abraham to the death of Jesus the Christ. This is clear proof that as descendants of slaves, our roots are found in Ancient Israel and not Africa. Furthermore, we should have nothing to do with Christianity whatsoever, since that philosophy is pagan and has no biblical foundation.

Finally, the word "Negro" originated with the Portuguese, meaning "black". Since there is no such country as "Negro", common sense should dictate that there can be no such person. Plus all black people of the world are NOT Israelites. In Portugal, the name "JEW" was changed to "Negro" when referring to our Israelite ancestors and has remained to this day. Let us correct this misnomer by returning to our proper identity. ISRAELITE IS OUR CULTURE, NATIONALITY, RELIGION AND PHILOSOPHY.

THE SILENCED ONE
By E. B. PORTER

VIOLENCE AGAINST WOMEN: A EUROCENTRIC MORALITY. *(Share Newspaper)* IS IT BECAUSE THEY'RE WOMEN? *(Toronto Star)* ARGUMENT OVER A WOMAN. *(Discover Magazine)* WOMEN IN FEAR. *(Macleans Magazine/Cover Article)* ARE WOMEN AN ENDANGERED SPECIES? *(Caribbean Camera).* Why do these headlines continue to appear in our newspapers? Is there a reason why women feel the way they do? Are we just spouting off emotion? Is there any validity in our cries? Is there justification for our frustrations?

I ask you to come with me on a historical journey. I shall attempt to tell the other side of the story - to explore another perspective - to uncover those hidden facts about our society and its effect on women, past and present. It is my desire that after you have read this chapter, you will better understand why these headlines fill our newspapers.

I cite two main reasons for the ongoing struggle of women. **Reason#1)** We lack the true knowledge, understanding and wisdom about ourselves. We do not understand our Creator, the God of Israel and how He made us. We yearn for the wisdom to function the way we were destined. We do not understand the mistakes we have made, the consequences of those errors and how we can right the wrongs. I, for one do not take the revelation I have received from the Israelites for granted and I hope I never will. I have strived for many years to understand who I am and my relationship to the Almighty Father. After hundreds of Christian sermons, studies, and years of bible school I was left with too many unanswered questions, especially in the areas of womanhood. My teachers of the past could not answer those many questions. How could they? The scriptures were not written for them to understand, let alone teach. The scriptures were written **only for the children of Israel.**

I cannot stress the importance of understanding the FIRST STORY, the story of creation, for the first few chapters of Genesis hold the keys to understanding **how** we were created, **why** we were created, **where** we went wrong, the consequences of those actions and **what** we can do about it.

The laws, statues and commandments laid down for the children of Israel; the beautiful stories of the great women of God, the warnings to us as women; to the instructions laid down by the apostle Paul are all there for us. The answers are in the bible, but without the revelation given to the children of Israel, taught by the children of Israel we will never, never fully understand ourselves and our roles. Only through this revelation will we have this feeling of completion and satisfaction deep within us.

Reason#2) The present upheaval is due to the fact that we live in a repressive and exploitative society. Let me make one thing clear from the beginning. **Any society where man plays God there will be oppression.** This would include the entire world, but I will not deal with an African, Oriental or Islamic culture, because we live in Canada and this society is based on "judeochristian" principles which gave birth in Europe. This is the culture I am addressing because it applies directly to our lives right here and right now.

Despite the progress over hundreds of years for different segments of the population this Christian society caters to an elite group of individuals - **the white Christian male** - with an inner circle of these certain men running the whole show. The rest of us struggle.

Through this brief historic overview, I will go back to a particular time in history, when the foundation stones of our modern society were being laid. I will try to uncover some of the causes for our present day dilemma concerning women.

For those of you who know me
Let us face the cold, hard FACTS!!!

The place is Europe. The time is between the 15th and 17th centuries. A tumultuous period for the entire continent. The ancient structures of tribal Europe were about to disintegrate. A wave of revolution had begun to pound upon Europe's shores. A force so strong as to destroy an entire way of life and set up a **NEW WORLD ORDER.**

Women's lives were to be changed forever

Before they were tribal women functioning as co-leaders in their societies, counsellors, physicians, and visionaries. Their lives were filled with ceremony and celebration. **NO MORE, NO MORE, NO MORE!!!**

The Edomites (so-called Jews) are relentless in reminding the world of the holocaust during the Second World War. It was one of the first things I noticed after being away from Canada for eleven years. Every week a new movie or documentary on this particular holocaust. But today our focus will be on another holocaust. I call it...

THE SILENCED ONE
THE WOMEN'S HOLOCAUST

You will not find these following facts in any glorious T.V. production on the grandeur of European history and its great accomplishments. There are few written records, thus most of the voices have been silenced.

Who were the victims of this silenced holocaust and why? The high estimation is nine million, the low is seven million women and children were accused, convicted, tortured and murdered during this time. MILLIONS OF LIVES. 85% of them were women. Six generations of children saw their mothers burn at the stake. The smoke from the burning flesh filled the skies of Europe for three hundred years. The moans of the tortured and the screams of the dying were an intricate part of everyday life during the formation and development of this new society.

What awesome, mighty force could possibly inflict such evil upon a people? Who was this enemy?

The church of Rome... set up the Inquisition to enforce ITS will. Anyone who critized the church or held different beliefs were charged with heresy and convicted as criminals. Many of the accused were women. The Christian church and state branded them witches and condemned them as worshippers of the devil. An insidious terror began to rule women's lives. Why did the church target women for their reign of terror?

Because women were the greatest challenge and threat to the advancement of the church. The Christian church recognized the spiritual power and influence of the woman in society and therefore began to wield its evil force over them. Here is a basic outline of the progression instigated by the church of Rome to manipulate and control every aspect of a woman's life.

WOMAN - THE CARE GIVER

For thousands of years women had been the physicians and care givers of the people. Many medicines in modern pharmacies were first used by "the wise women" hundreds, thousands of years ago.

THE FIRST TARGET OF CONTROL
THE MIDWIVES

Notice how the church singled out the midwives. Is this not the most sacred of all professions for a woman? To aid in the bringing forth of a new life. Remember how God once used the Hebrew midwives in Egypt to save the male children, at the time of Moses, from death by the sword of the enemy. Do not ever underestimate the cunning and craftiness of the enemy! These evil and perverted clergymen knew exactly what they were doing. They had their strategy planned out from the beginning.

Midwives were denounced by the church

This was a cover up for the real issue. The real issue was control. It was and is the purpose of the church of Rome to replace God and control every man, woman and child from birth to death. The priests were extremely jealous of the position that a midwife held in society and felt this honour and gratitude should be exclusively for him and the church. They were jealous of the love and respect bestowed upon the midwife by the families she administered to. Men and women alike revered her sacred duty and in the minds of the clergy this threat to their power had to end, and end it did.

Midwives were denounced by the church because they eased the pain of labour which was in their view God's punishment to woman because of her sin.

A woman was now forced to leave her home to give birth. Her home; a place of comfort and familiarity, a place of laughter and love, where her husband, children and other loved ones waited for her. This would be replaced by a cold, dark, bare room with a plank for a bed and some straw for a pillow. The soothing hands of an experienced midwife would be no more. A few crude instruments and an uncompassionate "male doctor" and of course "the priest" were many times her only two witnesses. What did these men know of the pains of labour? How could they give support to her in one of the most vulnerable times in a woman's life. The most exciting and glorious event for any family was now turned into pain and fear. Where was her mother? Her sister? The wise women? The midwife? Can you imagine the anxiety and fear that gripped her soul. These men of the Christian church replaced her husband. Where was he? He was no longer permitted to witness the birth of his own child.

Did this process of control stop here?

New laws proclaimed that any woman who dared practised midwifery or dared cured without having studied in a formal institution was a witch and must die. Since most women were barred from university, the rise of the male medical profession was guaranteed.

The church stated that women interrupted God's will through birth control and must pay for their actions. Women had too much control over their own bodies, their own lives and their own destiny and it had to stop.

The church hired spies and the testimony of male doctors sent many women to their death. Those who were once colleagues working side by side were turned into enemies. Do you not see how the Christian church began to inflict suspicion, mistrust and fear among men and women? Creating a WEDGE between the sexes in the professional arena. This wedge has become so ingrained into the culture that we feel the effects of this manipulation even today. Their roots are firmly entrenched into the psyche of this society.

The history books call this period of upheaval **THE WITCH CRAZE**. A devised programme of propaganda was unleashed upon the public to fear women. The most devastating aspect of our history is that the Christian church used the bible, an Israelite book as the means of justification for these insane actions.

I ASK YOU. Where were the Israelites to whom this word had been committed? I ASK YOU. Where was the Levite, the teachers of the gospel? The Nazarite, the defenders of the doctrine? I ASK YOU. Where were the twelve sons of Israel? They were being expelled from Europe by the thousands, and because of their disobedience and stiffnecked ways, they were scattered among the nations, carried about with every wind of doctrine, by the sleight of men, and cunning craftiness, falling into deep deception. They were shipped across the ocean as slaves, not knowing who they were and why this was happening, wishing they were dead.

AT THIS SAME TIME IN HISTORY THE ENEMY WAS AT WORK IN EUROPE STEALING THE ISRAELITE'S COLOURS, AND CLAIMING THE ISRAELITE BOOK, THE HOLY BIBLE FOR HIMSELF AND TURNING THE TRUTH INTO A LIE WITH DEVASTATING CONSEQUENCES THAT WOULD EFFECT THE ENTIRE WORLD. Now the power and influence of women to heal would only be associated with darkness, evil and destruction. HAD THE WORLD GONE CRAZY?

Every aspect of a woman's personal life was under attack. The Christian church fathers could not deal with a woman's individuality and spirituality. Any individual inspiration was a threat to the institutional church. This system of authority could not handle people such as Joan of Arc, who received personal revelation outside the church to lead the armies of France into battle, to bring peace to the land by having the Dauphin crowned King, Charles VII. After her victories, the surge of her popularity could not be quenched. Again, the clergy became frantic and jealous over her power and decided to brand her as a witch, and burned her at the stake in Rouen, France, May 30, 1431. Later in 1920 this same church declared Joan of Arc a saint. What utter confusion and hypocrisy.

Hundreds of women were herded into filthy prisons to await a mock trial. After days of hunger and cold they were stripped completely naked, shaved of all bodily hair, chained and brought before the Inquisition. They were dragged in backwards with no place to hide as these perverts feasted upon them with their eyes. False accusations were administered and if she did not confess to being a witch then she would undergo unbearable torture until she confessed. Sooner or later THEY ALL CONFESSED. For research purposes I forced myself to watch a number of films on the subject of the witch trials. They were horrific, beyond imagination and most of the time I could not finish watching them.

The rich were many times targeted. When the church needed money they would hire people, many times relatives or neighbours to falsely accuse these women of heresy. Some of the most famous women in Europe were burned at the stake, because of their beauty, wealth and power.

By the early 16th century a woman's right to own property was eroded. Long standing family names, properties and assets were lost forever. Most of the money was used to build shrines to the Queen of Heaven - the goddess Isis - (their Virgin Mary). Five hundred monstrosities/cathedrals were built in the space of 100 years - so they needed a lot of capital and knew where to get it.

THE HOME LIFE

Husbands were admonished from the pulpit to beat their wives. Men were taught into believing that women were the block to his holiness. Sexuality was no longer a gift, but the root of evil. Women were afraid to get old because the elderly women, who used to be revered as wise women, were killed by the thousands because of superstition. They were labelled as "hags." Before the Christian era a "hag" was "one with sacred knowledge." The church associated the word with age, ugliness and evil. Even today the word "hag" has negative connotations.

As I mentioned before the WEDGE already created by the Christian church in the professional field had edged its way between the sexes in their personal lives. Guilt, fear, and suspicion ruled most aspects of life. Men, because of fear, began to turn in their own wives to the authorities. Isn't it obvious? Everything positive about a woman was turned into a negative. The truth was turned into a lie. The lie became the truth. What a devastating process.

THE NEW CAPITALISM

The exploitation of women became big business during the rise of capitalism. The witch craze brought about many opportunities for employment. Lawyers, guards, accountants, executioners were all too willing to make a handsome profit from the suffering of thousands of women. As I said before, at this time the rich were especially targeted.

All the new and wonderful inventions coming forth from Europe were being welcomed throughout the world, but for many European women, the price of industrialization was paid with their blood.

THE PRINTING PRESS

A REVOLUTIONARY INVENTION that changed the world. Did you know that one of the first books to receive mass distribution, because of the invention of the printing press was called the **"MALLEUS MALE FICARUM"**. Top Ten Best Seller in the late 15th century. "Malius Malfaciera" THE HAMMER AGAINST WITCHES. It was the most popular handbook of interrogation. A pure study of repression and projection of male dominance over women. This book singled out women as the primary source of witchcraft. It was highly sexual and influential. This work was commissioned by Pope Innocent VIII, who hired two Dominican priests to document and invent all, and any kind of torture that could be used to make a woman confess. These men who were deprived of any natural sexual relations were given this task, so you can imagine what they came up with. **PERVERT** IS A MILD ADJECTIVE TO DESCRIBE THESE PRIESTS.

Do not ever be deceived by the painted masterpieces depicting these so-called holy fathers of the Christian church. THEY ARE ALL LIES. GUILTY, GLUTTON and a WINEBIBBER are more appropriate TITLES for POPE INNOCENT VIII. He was responsible for unspeakable atrocities toward mankind, especially women and he is an abomination to history itself. Alas, the history books were written by those in control. But there are a few of us who are determined to change that, and speak and write about the truth.

Do not be deceived - the effects of this period of history are still with us today because the foundation was built on oppression. Deep rooted attitudes passed down from generation to generation at times pervade our thinking and affect our actions.

Great strides and sacrifices have been made by numerous movements and groups of people down through the centuries, who protested against the Catholic Church - from the time of Luther to the modern day Evangelical movement - **all these believed that they were in protest.**

BUT THIS IS THE AWESOME DECEPTION AND I SPEAK FROM PERSONAL EXPERIENCE AS A FORMER CHRISTIAN MISSIONARY. ***THOSE IN PROTEST UP TO THIS DAY REMAIN UNDER THE SAME CURSED SYSTEM.*** An awesome deception for thousands of people, including my dearest friends and colleagues of the past who sincerely believe they are doing the right thing.

"WHEREFORE COME OUT FROM AMONG THEM, AND BE YE SEPARATE, SAITH THE LORD GOD, AND TOUCH NOT THE UNCLEAN THING, AND I WILL RECEIVE YOU, AND WILL BE A FATHER UNTO YOU, AND YE SHALL BE MY SONS AND DAUGHTERS, SAITH THE LORD ALMIGHTY." This is the God of Abraham, Isaac and Jacob speaking to the children of Israel.

The revelation of John speaks loud and clear of the GREAT WHORE representing the present day Christian system (including all Protestant movements) who sits upon many waters, which are multitudes of peoples, and nations and tongues, with one great city reigning over the kings of the earth. Her influence is all encompassing.

For those who doubt if these historical events have any bearing on women's lives today. I will state the following facts. In their latest report Stats Canada states that FOR THE SAME JOB women still receive only 67% of a man's salary. Midwifery remains unrecognized as an official profession in most parts of North America.

Female enrolment in the sciences remain well below that of their male colleagues, and we will not forget the massacre in Montreal where female engineering students were murdered by some psycho who had a grudge against women.

The exposure of sexual harassment and abuse against women and children is a **power** problem - an issue of control and violence. The ongoing exploitation of women in the T.V., film, and literature is blatant with huge profits in the making. I do not think I have to go on. IT IS OBVIOUS.

This is the burden we bear. WE CANNOT CHANGE THE PAST. We live in a society where man has replaced God's laws with his own. It is indelibly stamped upon our nature, a trait of Lucifer himself to want to be God, to play God. The world's political and philosophical systems are just an extension, a working out of human nature.

Even the Israelites cried out... "We want a King to rule over us." " WE WANT TO BE LIKE OTHER NATIONS." One of the most disturbing scriptures in the bible. They too wanted to live under man's rule instead of choosing the God of Israel as their Supreme Leader and to follow His instructions. Note the consequences of that choice.

Wisdom, freedom, respect, honour, protection, prosperity, fulfilment. Is this what we want as women?

I quote... "Man/Woman know thyself. Knowledge is power. Wisdom is strength. Understanding is the essence of life itself." Know your God, the God of Abraham, Isaac and Jacob. Know yourself, your strengths and your weaknesses. Know His laws, statues and commandments. Know and be confident in what you personally have to do.

THIS MAN MADE CHRISTIAN SYSTEM HAS OPPRESSED US, KEPT US IN IGNORANCE AND UTTERLY FAILED US AS WOMEN. BUT THANK GOD ALMIGHTY THERE IS AN ALTERNATIVE. **The path of the Israelites**. I say as an acting participant in the building of THE NATION OF ISRAEL. Let the God of ABRAHAM, ISAAC AND JACOB rule over us.

Under the shadow of the Almighty will I be protected
Obeying His law is my safeguard
In adhering to His council will my path in life be revealed

THE HEART OF A WOMAN
By Lina Vescio

I was raised to believe that every good Italian girl would grow up, get married, cook, clean and have children. And when married adhere to whatever her husband says whether it be right or wrong. I was raised to believe that a woman's place is behind her husband. I was raised to believe that a woman even though she was married, should not enjoy the pleasures of marriage, the pleasure is for the man alone. And if a man had a mistress he would be congratulated by his male peers. However, if a woman even dared to look at another man or remarked that a man was attractive, or far worse if a man even looked at her and she was aware of him looking at her, she would be beaten and then probably raped, by her own husband. This was very common among some Italian marriages at one time, and I'm sure to some degree still to this day. I was raised to believe that you could not, as woman be anywhere near intelligent as your husband. Some Italian women were beautiful but stupid. BUT THEN I WAS RAISED A CATHOLIC.

Just before I was married my brother-in-law-to-be decided he would lecture me on what percent of myself I should be giving to our marriage. I listened very carefully. He said in his family Fifty-Fifty does not exist. Sixty-Forty existed. Sixty for the man and Forty for the woman and that is how my husband and I should base our marriage. What he was really trying to say was sixty percent of the power to be the man's. Should there be a power struggle in a marriage? Italian marriages for the most part functioned in this manner. So the husbands were dominant and the women were submissive. However, something happened to these women. Some of them were still submissive but worked behind their husband's back. In turn they obtained whatever their hearts desired without their husbands even knowing it. This was a form of rebellion. Women would band together and discuss between one another how they cheated their husbands. Essentially this behaviour was then taught by some mothers to their daughters.

"YOU MUST OBEY YOUR HUSBAND."

However, if there was something that you really were after, mothers would teach their daughters to use their sexuality. This was a woman's only tool to achieve and deceive.

You see this chapter is not to bring forth the superiority in women or to ostracize men. But to educate or should I say re-educate ourselves regarding women and their role in society. I may sound like a "feminist." But I am not. It is not on society in general that I am basing my comments, but the role we play in society in assisting our men in shaping the foundation of this new nation of Israel, for the world to see. It is written that the world must see Israel rise. Yes, I do agree with the fact that it is a "man's world" and no, God is not a woman. However, let us not forget that the God of our fathers made us right along side our men. We did not come into the picture centuries after, but at creation. This issue is of great importance and must be addressed delicately. For if we are not careful in educating ourselves and our children according to the laws that our God has laid down for us, it could be to our detriment. Throughout this chapter please do not ignore the fact that as Israelites we have been blessed with the eyes to see the truth, which is written in our book, our bible, which is for men and women. Once we understand this point we will be able to focus with an open mind to the issues raised regarding women.

The doctrine was given to the children of Israel. But at one time Christianity and the Church of Rome took that doctrine and concealed it from men and women and extracted whatever it deemed beneficial for their triumphant success. Ah yes, they were successful, but for how long?

My mother used to tell me that the Pope knew the truth of our destiny because it was written in a secret book hidden in the Vatican. According to my mother, in her time, Italians were forbidden to read the bible. It was considered a sin. Nuns, I was told when I was a little girl, were severely punished up until the early 70's if they were caught reading the Holy Bible. They were beaten, put to work by scrubbing toilets and floors and given practically nothing to eat until they collapsed and confessed to reading the forbidden book, "The Holy Bible."

Reading the bible was considered sinful for the ordinary or undistinguished individual. The only distinguishable persons were the Hierarchy within the Catholic church and they were men. To some degree I think my mother was right, the few did know the truth, but the truth was suppressed in order to keep the masses ignorant, so power and control would reign within the church. Evidently the church was victorious in suppressing the masses, for there was extreme poverty in and around Europe. You are well aware of what happens to society once it is in a state of destitution. There is no difference today. The United States and Canada are falling apart at the seams and people are calling unto God for help, and Christianity is right there ready to swallow them up again, because of their vulnerability. Most Italians based their lives around the Catholic church and would give gold, money, salami, chickens, eggs by placing them either around the statue of the so-called Virgin Mary, or their favourite saint, or just handed it over to their town priests. In return the people would attain promises from these priests that some saint was watching over them. Which explains why the Catholic Church is the richest church in the world. But now there is the offspring of Catholicism, which are the Evangelical Christian Churches. There is no difference. Therefore, in retrospect it is not really man that suppressed woman throughout time, but Christianity.

Getting back to my youth and how I was raised. I was simply deceived. My mother should have been telling me how great it was to be a woman. What a great gift God gave me in bringing forth leaders, scholars and women of substance. Before getting married she should have explained how important it was to be along side my husband because with my assistance we could accomplish anything. Instead she cried in anguish and expressed sorrow and pity because I was born a woman and must endure pain in being a woman.

Oh yes, we did commit the first sin. But do we not pay for that every time we give birth to a child? And is it not paying for that sin when we become unclean through our monthly cycle most of our adult life? Must we continuously be suppressed because of our gender? And is not the doctrine of Israel meant for us as well? Who was the bible written for, man alone? No, it was written for the children of Israel who consisted of men and women. God laid down the laws to protect men from men and believe it or not women from men.

In the book of **<u>Deuteronomy 22:23-29</u>** "If a damsel that is a virgin be betrothed unto an husband, and a man find her in the city, and lie with her; Then ye shall bring them both out unto the gate of that city, and ye shall stone them with stones that they die; the damsel, because she cried not, being in the city; and the man, because he hath humbled his neighbour's wife: so thou shall put away evil from among you. But if a man find a betrothed damsel in the field, and the man force her, and lie with her: then the man only that lay with her shall die. But unto the damsel thou shall do nothing; there is in the damsel no sin worthy of death: for as when a man riseth against his neighbour, and slayeth him, even so is this matter: For he found her in the field, and the betrothed damsel cried, and there was none to save her. If a man find a damsel that is a virgin which is not betrothed, and lay hold on her, and lie with her, and they be found; Then the man that lay with her shall give unto the damsel's father fifty shekels of silver, and she shall be his wife; because he hath humbled her, he may not put her away all his days."

This scripture clearly states that if two people are engaged in activities not accepted by the God of Israel, then they both will be put to death. However, if a young girl is defiled then the man shall either be put to death or will have to marry her. This is the God of Israel protecting his young damsels. **<u>Numbers 27:1-8</u>** "Then came the daughters of Zelophehad, the son of Hepher, the son of Gilead, the son of Machir, the son of Manasseh, of the families of Manasseh the son of Joseph: and these are the names of his daughters; Mahlah, Noah, and Hoglah, and Milcah, and Tirzah. And they stood before Moses, and before Eleazar the priest, and before the princes and all the congregation, by the door of the tabernacle of the congregation, saying, Our father died in the wilderness, and he was not in the company of them that gathered themselves together against the Lord in the company of Korah; but died in his own sin, and had no sons. Why should the name of our father be done away from among his family, because he hath no son?

Give us therefore a possession among the brethren of our father. And Moses brought their cause before the Lord. And the Lord spake unto Moses, saying, The daughters of Zelophehad speak right: thou shalt surely give them a possession of an inheritance among their father's brethren; and thou shalt cause the inheritance of their father to pass unto them. And thou shalt speak unto the children of Israel, saying, If a man die, and have no son, then ye shall cause his inheritance to pass unto his daughter." Would God Himself have spoken to Moses if the women in Israel had no importance? I think not. Again I say the Lord our God is our protector and I give Him thanks for I am truly blessed to know Him.

There were many women in Israel that were favoured by our Creator. **Judges 4:4** speaks of the prophetess Deborah. Not only was Deborah a prophetess and judge in Israel at that time, but God's plan was completely fulfilled at the hand of Jael, Heber's wife (**Judges chapter 4**). And did not our God give us the greatest gift of all - to bear sons.

Please do not misunderstand me, I am not addressing this issue for women in general. But this issue will continuously arise unless both men and women in the House of Israel know their respective place.

Women in the House of Israel must edify themselves in the role they will play alongside their men. The answers are written in our book. The first step is take all our upbringing and idiosyncrasies, place them in a box in our mind and store them for reference only.

We have a function to fulfill. God has clearly stipulated this fact in the book of Genesis. As earlier stated, once we fully understand the story of the first creation, then we are on the right track.

Not only are we, the women who are fortunate to know the truth about the children of Israel capable of greatness, but we can also through our respective spirituality, ruin our men. So I entreat the women in Israel not to be so rapped up in spiritual matters. For instead of worshipping God you will discover yourself worshipping yourself. So what is our goal? I have a son and I have a daughter what shall I do? I am an Israelite. I follow the instructions given by the God of Israel.

A little girl should not feel cursed because she was born a female. This is where education is vital. Teaching them that their femininity is eminent. To build their self-esteem. To prepare them for motherhood for that is the most beautiful endowment that God has given us. To bring forth life. To be strong. Physically we know women are very strong. They can endure much pain. But strength must also come from within. Strength in keeping silent, sometimes even when you know your spouse or your partner is at fault. Only a foolish woman reprimands her husband in public. We must stand beside our men in shaping this foundation of the House of Israel here in Canada, then eventually the world.

Proverbs 14:1 says, "Every wise woman buildeth her house: but the foolish plucketh it down with her hands." This is exactly what we must do as wise women, build our house and make our foundation strong. We must be aware of our strengths and weaknesses, stand proud, raise our self-esteem, be confident that we are an important part of Israel and last but not least, go to the Almighty God for everything. He has the answers, the advice and the ability to make you a great woman, through Him, the God of our Fathers, the God of Abraham, the God of Isaac and the God of Jacob.

THE ARK OF THE COVENANT
KNOWN ALSO AS THE ARK OF THE LORD
THE ARK OF GOD
AND THE ARK OF HIS TESTAMENT

By Shadrock

It is the goal of many archeologists, university professors, the media and even the centre of many movie plots, to obtain the knowledge and understanding of this very important topic.

The Webster New Collegiate dictionary explains The Ark Of The Covenant as being "a sacred chest representing to the Hebrews, the presence of God among them; which contains the ten commandments."

It is said by some, that this once most precious symbol, lies somewhere in a temple in Ethiopia tended by a lone priest, and no one is allowed to see this ark. This is nothing else but a myth, and must be treated as a lie. That is why he is a lone priest and no one can see this ark, because it does not exist. This is a story circulated around to fit the cause of some, who are begging for a place in history. If there is such a lonely man, he was probably placed there by someone, or group to watch the biggest lie ever. **There is no such thing as The Ark Of The Covenant in Ethiopia**. This is a cursed land, also the inheritor of the Egyptian gods, the ENEMY of the TRUE AND LIVING GOD. They were on the side of Egypt who was against the children of Israel and their God. Egypt and Ethiopia were of the same culture, and ruled by over twenty of the same rulers. Besides, all this ridiculous rumour is a lot of hot air, blown around by the ignorant. God will never place such a holy thing in the land of the children of Ham.

According to the Holy Bible, Ethiopians were always different from God's people in their philosophy, not skin and hair texture, but today all you ever hear about is Egypt and Ethiopia. People are confused when they read the scripture that says that princes shall come out of Egypt, Ethiopia shall soon stretch forth her hand unto God, **Psalms 68:31**.This scripture is reminding us that the children of Israel (who are princes) did come out of

Egypt. Ethiopia will turn from her worshipping of multiple gods like the Egyptians, and turn to the one true and living God, the God of Abraham Isaac and Jacob.

Ezekiel 30:4-5 "And the sword shall come upon Egypt, and great pain shall be in Ethiopia, when the slain shall fall in Egypt, and they shall take away her multitude, and her foundations shall be broken down. Ethiopia, and Libya, and Lydia, and all the mingled people, and Chub, and the men of the land that is in league, shall fall with them by the sword."

Ezekiel 38 tells of all those who are the enemies of God and surely Ethiopia is among them in the **fifth verse**, along with Gog and Magog and Egypt and Libya. **Nahum 3:1-10** will also explain the difference between the people of the land called Ethiopia, and the Ethiopians spoken about in **Amos 9:7** "Are ye not as children of the Ethiopians unto me, O children of Israel? saith the Lord. Have I not brought up Israel out of the land of Egypt? and the Philistines from Caphtor, and the Syrians from Kir?"

Here is where the scripture is identifying the likeness of the children of Israel. The bible is not saying that the Ethiopians are the children of Israel, or have the same status, because it also gives the difference with the statement "Are ye not as children of the Ethiopians?" If I should say are you not like the children of Africa, O' children of slaves? The answer would be yes. Note the names mentioned in the verse; Egypt, Ethiopia, Syria, Philistines, etc. All these did battle with God as His enemy.

The children of Israel were black with woolly hair just like the Ethiopians. There was no such word as African then. Woolly haired people were called Ethiopians, then later on, by the name of their country and their father's name. It has absolutely nothing to do with the land Ethiopia as we know it today. The word African replaced the word Ethiopian.

The proof is written in the bible. God's enemies came from the seed of Ham. As black as they were, they were still His enemies. The Egyptians, the Ethiopians, the Canaanites, the Philistines and all that dwell in their land. **I Chronicles 1:8** "The sons of Ham; **Cush** and Mizraim, **Put,** and **Canaan. Verse 12** states "And Pathrusim, and Casluhim, (of **whom came the Philistines,**) and Caphthorim"

The Ethiopians of Ethiopia are described in **Zephaniah 2:12**.

"Ye Ethiopians also, ye shall be slain by my sword." To understand the difference you must read **Isaiah 20, 43:3, 45:14.** The people who are circulating this vicious lie that Ethiopia is God's country, worship an Ethiopian ruler, who renamed himself to gain favour and popularity, clinging to a title that would transform him into being some sort of a legend or god. He followed closely in the footsteps of another one who also named himself Menelik II.

JUDGE FOR YOURSELF.

Earlier, in 1000 BC. there was a link between the Arabian Peninsula and what is now called Ethiopia. In the next 1000 years, people from southwestern Arabia migrated to northern Ethiopia and later this kingdom was known as Aksum. In this same era it was said that an Ethiopian princess named Makeda (Queen of Sheba) visited Solomon, king of Israel and bore him a son called Menelik. In the fourth century AD. Christianity was the sole and recognized philosophy in the land of Ethiopia. For 1000 years Ethiopia was cut off from the outside world. There was bitter infighting among the leadership, and religion played a major role in this sea of confusion.

In the midst of the 19th century Ethiopia began to show her face again, a face marred with battle scars. Between the rubble of the pillars of this kingdom came forth Towodros II. The British attacked Ethiopia during his rule, and he committed suicide. Again more confusion. Then came a leader with the smarts to outwit them all. He called himself Menelik II. A Christian, a great admirer of the Christian fathers of Rome.

After about 1000 years in the B.C. era, followed by almost another 2000 years A.D. this man appeared: What happened to the original Menelik's heir three thousand years ago? What happened to three thousand years? He was also trying to have a line of rulers named after him, with the name he stole "Menelik" This act of naming or renaming oneself is a pagan practice and no man of God was ever instructed to do so.

Menelik eventually messed it all up when he placed his entire country in the hands of the Italians, who then seized a part of Eritrea. So fell his dream of the resurrection of the name Menelik. The people lost faith in him. Then the son of Makonen whose real name was Ras Tafari Makonen took over leadership, and before you know it, he too changed his name to gain favour of the people, he did not call himself Menelik, but worse; "king of kings

93

and lord of lords," "conquering lion of the tribe of Judah." This very man was a devout Christian who belonged to the Ethiopian Christian church, a branch of the Egyptian Coptic church. How can an Ethiopian Christian, who professes to be from the tribe of Judah be telling the truth? He is confused already, by trying to embrace conflicting philosophies as one. You must be one or the other, a Christian or a Jew, not both. Somebody must be lying. Nebuchadnezzar, the Babylonian king was also called king of kings. **Daniel 2:37 "Thou, O king, art a king of kings..."** In the book of Esther, you would find another Babylonian Ethiopian ruler, who ruled Ethiopia. His name was **AHASUERUS. Esther 1:1** "Now it came to pass in the days of Ahasuerus, (this is Ahasuerus which reigned, from India even unto Ethiopia, over an hundred and seven and twenty provinces:)"

It was the self-named **Menelik II** who copied or took the colours from the Romans and the Babylonians. The Ethiopian colours of **RED, GREEN** and **YELLOW** (gold is a mineral and not a colour) were copied from the Babylonian empire. You will find it in **Esther 1:6** "Where were white, green, and blue, hangings, fastened with cords of fine linen and purple to silver rings and pillars of marble: the beds were of gold and silver, upon a pavement of red, and blue, and white and black, marble."

He discarded the colours of the Hebrews. Do you think that the God of Abraham, Isaac and Jacob would put one of His most treasured symbols, meant for the children of Israel, in the hands of their enemy, the Ethiopians? Never!

Then there are others who wish not to be outdone. They need to rechannel or rather redirect this belief, so that it would never get out of their clutches. They cannot allow others to believe that this precious little box, (God's little box) could be in anyway connected to black people. So they started their own little rumour, "It's in Jerusalem." This would sound better, for every bible toting Christian would believe it. They would prefer to swallow a camel rather than not believe.

It is time we turn to the scriptures to find out what God and His prophets have to say about this matter, for it is the nature of man to lie, to impress other men in order to suppress and oppress them through philosophy.

Exodus 25 explains how, when, where and for whom the Ark was built. You will discover **Verse four** mentions the colours of the Israelites. *"And Blue and Purple and Scarlet and Fine Linen..."* (fine linen means white). Please note the surroundings would have to be consistent with everything including the colours of God, not red, green, black and yellow. **Verse 2** tells who God was speaking to, and about, "Speak unto the children of Israel..." - not Israelis, Edomites, Egyptians, Ethiopians or Gentiles. The other two chapters deal with specific instructions for the making of the Ark, and the Tabernacle and their purpose.

The caretakers of the Ark were chosen by God Himself from among the tribe of Levi. **Numbers 3:30-31** "And the chief of the house of the father of the families of the Kohathites shall be Elizaphan the son of Uzziel. And their charge shall be the ark..."

You will notice in the following verse how serious it was to go against this command of God. **II Samuel 6:6-7** "And when they came to Nachon's threshingfloor, Uzzah put forth his hand to the ark of God, and took hold of it; for the oxen shook it. And the angel of the Lord was kindled against Uzzah; and God smote him there for his error; and there he died by the ark of God."

Christians and Israelis alike are claiming that this Ark was buried by Rabbis in some cave in Jerusalem before the Babylonians came. This is a lie that has no taste, and should not be digested by any person with average intelligence.

Let's examine the purpose of the Ark of God. **Numbers 10:35** "And it came to pass, when the ark set forward, that Moses said, Rise up Lord, and let thine enemies be scattered; and let them that hate thee flee before thee."

In other words the ark was used by the children of Israel as a weapon to fight for them. Yet today the world is swallowing such a huge lie that the Israelites hid the ark to prevent it from getting damaged when the Babylonians came, thus making the God of Abraham, Isaac and Jacob a wimp, God forbid, when He is not.

Dear reader, would you hide your most effective weapon in a time of battle? Would it have been a wise decision for the Americans to have hidden the Patriot from Iraq's scud missile? If your answer is no, then you will see how stupid it sounds, hiding the ark from the enemy. Let us remember that at one point, the enemy did have control of the ark. The purpose was really to teach the children of Israel a lesson about obedience. Because of their disobedience, or as the bible so cleverly puts it "because of their stiffnecked ways" they lost it to their enemies.

I Samuel 5 gives a graphic report. The return of the Ark can be found in the next chapter. **I Samuel 6**. The reason for its return? It did not work in the hands of the enemy. This is additional proof of the stupidity of the explanation given by fools.

Let us follow the path taken by the Ark in its last days. **II Chronicles 35:3** "And said unto the Levites that taught all Israel, which were holy unto the Lord, Put the holy ark in the house which Solomon the son of David king of Israel did build; it shall not be a burden upon your shoulders: serve now the Lord your God and his people Israel."

According to scripture the children of Israel were no longer in the wilderness, they were now in the land which the Lord their God gave to them - not the Israelis, the Israelites. Solomon did put the Ark in its final resting place in Jerusalem along with the Tabernacle of the congregation with all its vessels, because it was Solomon that was commanded by God to do this job. **II Chronicles 6:9**. "Notwithstanding thou shalt not build the house; but thy son which shall come forth out of thy loins, he shall build the house for my name."

I Kings 8:9 "There was nothing in the ark save the two tables of stone, which Moses put there at Horeb, when the Lord made a covenant with the children of Israel, when they came out of the land of Egypt." No covenant was made with the Israelis, Egyptians, Ethiopians or Christians for that matter. Now that we read what was in the Ark, what comes next?

Jeremiah 3:15-16 "And I will give you pastors according to mine heart, which shall feed you with knowledge and understanding. And it shall come to pass, when ye be multiplied and increased in the land, in those days, saith the Lord, **they shall say no more, The ark of the covenant of the Lord: neither shall it come to mind: neither shall they remember it; neither shall they visit it; neither shall that be done any more.**"

The above scripture is the word of the Lord, making all other statements null and void. For God did not need a house to dwell in, He made all things. The Ark of the covenant was built to prove to the children of Israel the power of our God. It was built to show wonders at the river Jordan. It was also built to draw them together in a single accord, to teach them how to be obedient and follow instructions laid down by Him through His Servants and His Prophets, for God resides in the heavens. **Acts 7:47-48** "But Solomon built him an house. Howbeit the most High dwelleth not in temples made with hands; as saith the prophet,"

There should be no more argument on this matter. The people who are spreading these lies, should shut up once and for all. Nothing about the "Cherub" or "Cherubims" should be uttered from the lips of these unqualified teachers. Because it is mentioned in the bible, that God spoke from between the two cherubims above the Ark, every Christian preacher is ready and willing to give his or her version of it. God never spoke to a Christian about these matters, yet today they take hold of the authority to teach. The Cherubims were different when they were placed in the Garden of Eden, in **Genesis 3:24** from **Exodus 25:17-22.** It was different again when He rode upon it in **II Samuel 22:10-11**. The huge one made in **I Kings 6:23-28**. The difference again is in the book of **Ezekiel 41:17-19**. Even Lucifer was an anointed Cherub in **Ezekiel 28:14**.

How come the English dictionary says the meaning of Cherub or Cherubims is "a little winged baby"? This white winged baby is painted all over the Catholic, and other Christian churches Where did they get their authority from? Was God riding this baby in **II Samuel**? Did this baby have wheels as written in **Ezekiel 10**? Paul said that we are not even allowed to discuss this highly spiritual subject. Yet these Christian preachers are playing little gods, and lying, even denouncing Paul their teacher? **Hebrews 9:3-5** "And after the second veil, the tabernacle which is called the Holiest of all; Which had the golden censer, and the ark of the covenant overlaid round about with gold, wherein was the golden pot that had manna, and Aaron's rod that budded, and the tables of the covenant; **And over it the cherubims of glory shadowing the mercyseat; of which we cannot now speak particularly.**"

The conclusion of this whole matter is very clear, the Ark of God is no longer in existence upon this earth. Even if it did exist up to 70 A.D. when the Romans came. They destroyed Jerusalem and they made quite sure that no temple or symbol or mark was left standing. History states they destroyed all the temples in Jerusalem.

The ark is now symbolic as the Garden of God, or as paradise. **<u>Revelation 11:15-19</u>** "And the seventh angel sounded; and there were great voices in heaven, saying, The kingdoms of this world are become the kingdoms of our Lord, and of his Christ; and he shall reign for ever and ever. And the four and twenty elders, which say before God on their seats, fell upon their faces, and worshipped God, Saying, We give thee thanks, O Lord God Almighty, which art, and wast, and art to come; because thou hast taken to thee thy great power, and hast reigned. And the nations were angry, and thy wrath is come, and the time of the dead, that they should be judged, and that thou shouldest give reward unto thy servants the prophets, and to the saints, and them that fear thy name, small and great; and shouldest destroy them which destroy the earth. **And the temple of God was opened in heaven, and there was seen in his temple The ark of his testament; and there were lightnings, and voices, and thunderings, and an earthquake, and great hill.**"

Have you concluded? If you did, what is your conclusion? Those who have ears to hear let them hear. Remember any fool can claim knowledge, but only the wise can really attain it, only the wise can have the understanding of truth. And the truth is, there is no Ark of the Covenant in either the land called Israel today, or in Ethiopia. According to the scriptures, it is now in the heavens, the dwelling place of the Most High, the Holy One of Israel. The Israelites today are no longer together as a nation to take care of God's Holy Ordinances, and things. He would never leave such a holy symbol in the hands of the enemy. Never!

WHOSE UNDER GRACE?

We hear so much today about grace. What is grace? Where does it come from? Who is under it? What role does it play in gaining salvation? Does anyone need grace?

This can of worms must be opened very carefully. We cannot afford for one worm to escape, because to some, the revealing of this little secret is going to upturn their apple-cart and expose their spoiled fruits, and the bible says you shall know them by their fruit. So let's open the can of worms, catch them all back and give them to the owners who well deserve them. They had them for nearly two thousand years, and didn't know what to do with them.

Grace is like unto a light that lights a path. It is also like a honeycomb that attracts the bees. Grace is like food for the hungry. Grace is the riches of the Holy. It is wealth to the children of God. There is a rather simple way to explain the meaning of grace.

In the world of material wealth, the rich man gives to the poor. It is through the rich man's wealth that the poor man may be satisfied. The poor man may even become rich also, if he uses the money he receives from the rich man wisely. Therefore it would be safe to say, that the poor man can be made rich through the generosity of the rich man, but the source of the rich man's wealth is not known to the poor man.

Grace is that light that can save the heathen and the Gentiles. Grace is that source that can save the world, but it is only given by an Israelite, because he is the rich man. He gets his riches by keeping the laws, the statutes and the commandments. The heathen and the Gentile would get their riches through him.

In other words, the Israelites are always under the law, the law is their source. The Gentile would be under grace, because they are not of the circumcision, and they were not chosen by God. There is no promise made between God and anyone else except the children of Israel. Only fools will teach that there is no more law, for if there is no law, then there will be no judgment. It is a broken law that warrants punishment.

This confusion was started by the teachings of unqualified teachers of the new testament, by people who are ignorant of God's truth.

When the bible speaks of grace in terms of salvation it is always in the books of Paul. All Paul is ever saying is, that through Christ anyone can have grace, because He (Jesus the Christ) came full of grace. We must prove that Jesus the Christ came full of grace. **Zechariah 12:10** "And I will pour upon the house of David, and upon the inhabitants of Jerusalem, **the spirit of grace and of supplications**: and they shall look upon me whom they have pierced, and they shall mourn for him, as one mourneth for his only son, and shall be in bitterness for him, as one that is in bitterness for his firstborn."

John 1:14-17 "And the Word was made flesh, and dwelt among us, (and we beheld his glory, the glory as of the only begotten of the Father,) **full of grace and truth**. John bare witness of him, and cried saying, This was he of whom I spake, He that cometh after me is preferred before me: for he was before me. **And of his fullness have all we received, and grace for grace. For the law was given by Moses, but grace and truth came by Jesus Christ.**" And the truth is Jesus was an Israelite.

To understand the meaning of this scripture, is to understand that Moses was given the law for the children of Israel. Jesus himself being an Israelite, was born within the law. He came full of grace, so that anyone else could gain salvation through Him. That is why it is mentioned in the scriptures that you cannot go to the Father but by me (the Christ). We will prove that no one except an Israelite can gain salvation direct from God.

This is best explained when Paul spoke to Gentiles in **Ephesians 2:1-10. Verses 1&2** "And you hath he quickened, who were dead in trespasses and sins; Wherein in time past ye walked according to the course of this world, according to the prince of the power of the air, the spirit that now worketh in the children of disobedience:" The children of disobedience are the Israelites.

If we should stop here for a while, and read this over we will find that this is not a general statement. The children of the circumcision today are ignorant of their blessings. The uncircumcised Gentile is now in full control of a substitute they believe to be God. It looks good and is putting bread on their table.

The children of God are now running to these Gentiles for help. They fill the Christian churches and swallow up the false doctrines. The children of slavery, like their fathers before them, have a zeal to worship, but not of truth and righteousness. **Romans 10:1-3** "Brethren, my heart's desire and prayer to God for Israel is, that they might be saved. For I bear them record that they have a zeal of God, but not according to knowledge. For they being ignorant of God's righteousness, and going about to establish their own righteousness, have not submitted themselves unto the righteousness of God."

Ephesians 2:3-9 "Among whom also we all had our conversation in times past in the lusts of our flesh, fulfilling the desires of the flesh and of the mind; and were by nature the children of wrath, even as others. **But God, who is rich in mercy, for his great love wherewith he loved us, Even when we were dead in sins, hath quickened us together with Christ, (by grace ye are saved;) And hath raised us up together, and made us sit together in heavenly places in Christ Jesus:** That in the ages to come he might shew the exceeding riches of his grace in his kindness toward us through Christ Jesus. **For by grace are ye saved through faith; and that not of yourselves: it is the gift of God: Not of works, lest any man should boast."**

Let me repeat myself. We must find out from our teachers who is talking to whom, and please do not generalize statements written in the bible. They are strictly for, and about Israelites.

In the **third verse** Paul is reminding the Gentiles who they really were, the children of wrath. In **Verses 7&8** we notice the clearness and clarity of the underlined statement that the Gentiles cannot be saved by themselves, but by the grace of the Christ who was an Israelite, and through faith. The only way a Gentile and an Israelite can join together in Christ, is through the doctrine of Israel - not Christianity.

<u>**Galations 5:2-6**</u> "Behold, I Paul say unto you, that if ye be circumcised, Christ shall profit you nothing. **For I testify again to every man that is circumcised, that he is a debtor to do the whole law.** Christ is become of no effect unto you, **whosoever of you are justified by the law**; ye are fallen from grace. For we through the Spirit wait for the hope of righteousness by faith. For in Jesus Christ neither circumcision availeth anything, nor uncircumcision; but faith which worketh by love." This scripture is confirming the fact that there were those who were under the law by nature and by birth.

These happen to be the same scriptures the Christians read, but they have interpreted rather than demonstrate their understanding of this plain statement. If you are of the circumcision, you are not automatically saved, but you are however, automatically under the law. Breaking the law, or ignoring it, would have serious consequences.

The children of the circumcision have a job to do, and they cannot do it if they are living like Gentiles and not by the law laid down for them.

The lineage of the faith written about in the bible is that of the doctrine and practice of the Israelites. <u>**Ephesians 2:10**</u> "For we are his workmanship, created in Christ Jesus unto good works, which God hath before ordained that we should walk in them."

Here again is proof that Paul under the authority of the promise, through the blood of the circumcision is stating again that it was people like him (the Israelites) who were ordained from the start to carry out the assignment. In **Verses 11 & 12** there is another reminder of this misinterpreted scripture.

We will also discover in other scriptures that the grace spoken about in the scriptures are upon Israelites and can only be had by Gentiles through them, and not direct contact with God. <u>**Ephesians 3:8**</u> "Unto me, who am less than the least of all saints, is this grace given, that I should preach among the Gentiles the unsearchable riches of Christ;"

Hereby making the song "Amazing Grace" strictly for Gentiles, and no Israelite should utter it. We must understand the difference between the Israelites and the Gentiles, and the role the Gentiles play even today.

THE CHRISTIAN CHURCH
A GENTILE'S DREAM
OF SALVATION

What place do the Israelites take among the Gentiles? What is the difference between an Israelite and a Gentile? When these questions are answered fully, then and only then can this Christian myth be cleared up, which states that God has now chosen the Gentiles. This is yet another example of ignorance displayed by the Christian church. The major question is...has God turned His back on the Israelites? We have heard those proclaiming that the scriptures state that God has done away now with the Israelites and has now chosen the Christians and their philosophy. Let it be stated now and forever that according to the scriptures the philosophy of the Gentiles will never be accepted by God. Never!

We must prove that this statement is a lie. If this is true, then God is a liar, God forbid. He made an everlasting covenant with the children of Israel to be their God forever and ever. Is God a liar? No. The bible repeats this statement all the time, yet no one understands. Salvation is not of the Gentiles, but of the Jews. **John 4:22. Ezekiel 34:30-31**. <u>**Matthew 15:24**</u> "But he answered and said, I am not sent but unto the lost sheep of the **House of Israel.**"

Gentiles can only be saved by grace through faith in the doctrine of Israel, which was the doctrine of Jesus the Christ, who was an Israelite. All others, including Christianity are nothing but strange philosophies. The Christian church started, and is still being operated by Gentiles. The Gentiles are to Christianity what today's so-called Jews are to Judaism. They are both created by their practitioners, and have nothing to do with the doctrine of Israel (truth).

Isaiah 42:1-9. <u>**Verse 1**</u> "Behold my servant, whom I uphold; mine elect, in whom my soul delighteth; I have put my spirit upon him: *he shall bring forth judgment to the Gentiles.*"

The bible is confirming that the light or, the only way to salvation can only be through the doctrine of Israel.

Isaiah 42:6 "I the Lord have called thee in righteousness, and will hold thine hand, and will keep thee, and give thee for a covenant of the people, **for a light of the Gentiles;**" The book of the prophesy of Jesus the Christ, the prophet Isaiah states, that it is Israel that will give the light to the Gentiles.

Now if the Gentiles would have to get the word, the message, and the light from God's people, the Israelites, how come now the Gentiles are teaching the children of Israel? We must never forget that Christianity is not consistent with the instructions given in the holy bible. The deception lies in the fact that they too read the bible. There is however, absolutely no understanding of its contents. Their practice is a traditional pagan one. If I go to Rome, I would not know how to find my way around without a map of Rome or, I must ask a Roman to show me where I need to go. If you need God, you will have to ask an Israelite. The bible is the map of God. The God written about in the bible, is the God of Israel. **Verse 9** "Behold, the former things are come to pass, and new things do I declare: before they spring forth I tell you of them." How can anyone besides an Israelite know of things to come, or for that matter, know anything of God? This would be to directly go against the teachings of the doctrine.

Isaiah 49:6 "And he said, It is a light thing that thou shouldest be my servant to raise up the tribes of Jacob, and to restore the preserved of Israel: I will also give thee for a *light to the Gentiles*, that thou mayest be my salvation *unto the end of the earth*."

The scriptures explain the role the Gentiles played in the old testament and in the times of the prophets. That role was to follow, or to allow the children of Israel to lead them if they wanted salvation, because the children of Israel were the children of light. The Gentiles before had no knowledge of God, no power of the Holy Spirit.

Let us now find out if the new testament had changed all that. First, let us examine the life and purpose of Jesus the Christ, for this is where the Christians are trying to see their role. Notable through the books of Paul, which are being used in the interpretation of a belief suitable to their teachings.

<u>Acts 7:44-46</u> "Our fathers had the tabernacle of witness in the wilderness, as he had appointed, speaking unto Moses, that he should make it according to the fashion that he had seen. Which also our fathers that came after brought in with Jesus into the possession of the Gentiles, whom God drave out before the face of our fathers, unto the day of David. **Who found favour before God, and desired to find a tabernacle for the God of Jacob."**

In these few verses from the new testament, written by Paul, it states that God had cast aside the Gentiles because He had chosen Israel. Here Stephen is also crying out. Remember what you have been reading in the old testament that God has done for Israel. **Acts 9:11-18.** <u>Verse 15</u> "But the Lord said unto him, Go thy way: for he is a chosen vessel unto me, **to bear my name before the Gentiles**; and kings, and the children of Israel:"

The Lord is speaking here, not a man. Hence the beginning of the misunderstanding by teachers whose only conviction is to teach from the books of Paul. A man with two different messages, one for the Gentiles and another for his brethren. A man whose job was to teach Gentiles, and that is why the teachers of Christianity are so receptive of the doctrine for the Gentiles.

Christian preachers are making a terrible mistake by calling themselves "spiritual Israelites." This was the most enjoyable laugh I ever had when I first heard it. The Israelites were a nation of people, that are at present in their land of captivity - not spirits. God did not lead spirits out of Egypt. Neither did He chose spirits to be His children, but men and women, flesh and bones. Jacob was not a spirit. His children were not spirits. We are not spirits, and this term of "spiritual Jew" is not found anywhere in the bible. **Ezekiel 34:31** states that His people were men.

<u>Acts 10:41</u> *"Not to all the people, but unto witnesses chosen before of God, even to us, who did eat and drink with him after he rose from the dead."* Who ate and drank with Him? Were they spirits? When He returned He revealed Himself only to those witnesses chosen. The Israelites are the witnesses and chosen ones.

105

This is a symbol that when He returns again, He would go to those of the twelve from the House of Israel first. Unlike what Christians are saying today, that all are welcome, and that we are all children of God. This statement is not written anywhere in the holy bible.

Luke 1:1-80. **Verse 5** "There was in the days of Herod, the king of Judaea, a certain priest named Zacharias, of the course of Abia: and his wife was of the daughters of Aaron, and her name was Elisabeth."

This verse establishes the fact that the one who must prepare the way for the Messiah (Elijah) must be from the House of Israel, an Israelite from the tribe of the priesthood, a Levite. The story goes on to explain that Zacharias was of the priesthood and a Levite. His wife was also an Israelite.

Verses 15 & 16 "For he shall be great in the sight of the Lord, and shall drink neither wine nor strong drink; and he shall be filled with the Holy Ghost, even from his mother's womb. And many of the children of Israel shall he turn to the **Lord their God.**"

We understand from this scripture that John the Baptist could not have been a Lutheran, Baptist, Seventh Day Adventist, or a Jehovah Witness. He could not have been a Christian period, because Christians drink wine at their altars, or as some call it grape juice. Logic and common sense dictates that He could not have been a Christian, because he had the Holy Ghost with him, and if the Holy Ghost resides within any man he cannot drink wine. The scripture also personalized God. It did not say God, but the **Lord their God.** Not a god of the world.

Verse 17 "And he shall go before him in the spirit and power of Elias, (Elijah) to turn the hearts of the **fathers to the children, and the disobedient to the wisdom of the just: to make ready a people prepared for the Lord.**"

We must understand the segregation here. We now see why this child had to be born, and to whom he came. But this is just a chip of the ice-burg. John was just preparing the way. Let us get to know the person whose way he is preparing, Jesus the Christ. **Verse 27** "To a virgin espoused to a man whose name was Joseph, of the house of David; and the virgin's name was Mary." Joseph was an Israelite from the tribe of Judah, a Jew.

Verse 31-33 "And, behold, thou shalt conceive in thy womb, and bring forth a son, and shalt call his name JESUS. He shall be great, and shall be called the Son of the Highest: and the Lord God shall give unto him the throne of his father David: And he shall reign over the **house of Jacob for ever; and of his kingdom there shall be no end.**"

This Jew, this Israelite, conceived by this woman, shall rule over the house of Jacob, which is the House of Israel, forever - never taken away. We can stop here, and not have a single argument, if we have the spirit of understanding, but lo, I know that this spirit is a scarce commodity.

Verse 54-55 "He hath holpen his servant Israel, in remembrance of his mercy; **As he spake to our fathers, to Abraham, and to his seed for ever.**"

Again the covenant is established with the children of Israel forever, who today are the children of slavery. Just in case you lost track, this is the new testament. **Verse 68&69** "Blessed be the Lord God of **Israel**; for he hath visited and redeemed **his people**, And hath raised up an horn of salvation for us in the house of his servant David;"

Verse 80 "And the child grew, and waxed strong in spirit, and was in the deserts till the day of his shewing unto **Israel**." After reading these verses no one should be telling you that God has done away with the children of Israel.

Matthew 6:29-34. **Verse 32** "(For after all these things do the Gentiles seek:) for **your** heavenly Father knoweth that ye have need of all these things."

You do not have to be a lawyer to see the separation between the Israelites and the Gentiles. Note; "for your heavenly Father" specifying the Israelite's God. Here Jesus the Christ is speaking to the twelve disciples representing the twelve tribes of the House of Israel saying... "for after all these things do the Gentiles seek." That is why today the foolish things are so palatable because we are being indoctrinated by the doctrine of the Gentiles, who lay all the emphasis on LOVE, and material things and none on the spirit of TRUTH. Even some Israelites, due to the lack of knowledge call themselves Gentiles. "For your heavenly father..." which is different from the Gentile god. You may call this bible prejudice and you may be right because it is separating between God's people, the heathen, and the Gentiles. Why do people continue to say this bible is for the whole world. Can we not see the clear separation?

Romans 1:16 "For I am not ashamed of the gospel of Christ: for it is the power of God unto salvation to every one that believeth; to the Jews first, and also to the Greek." The Jew must lead, and others, including the Greek must follow. There should be no misunderstanding of this matter. The Jew first, and the Jew is an Israelite.

Revelation 11:2 "But the court which is without the temple leave out, and measure it not; for it is given unto the **Gentiles**: and the holy city shall they tread under foot forty and two months."

Is God really saying that the Gentiles will be in the outer court, and not welcome? You would also understand that this truth cannot be taught by a Christian who tells you every Sunday that God loves everyone. This is a very hard doctrine to teach. Would God take away a covenant that He had given to His people signed with the blood of their foreskins? No! He has not done that with any other people before, and He would not do that again.

Regardless of how bad your child is, he or she is still your child. When the fools have said that God has turned Himself away from Israel, you ask them if they would turn themselves away from their child, even if they were bad?

As **Psalm 77** says, we keep wondering because of the struggle, has God cast us off? Have we been put away forever? Is it that when we come back to God, He would not hear us? We must continue crying out to our God, the God of Abraham, the God of Isaac and the God of Israel, because He would hear our cry. There would have been no crying if there was no suffering. And if you read any psalms of Asaph you would find a cry for Israel.

Isaiah 54:1-10. Verses 5-7 "For thy maker is thine husband; the Lord of hosts is his name; and thy Redeemer the Holy One of Israel; the God of the whole earth shall he be called. For the Lord hath called thee as a woman forsaken and grieved in spirit, and a wife of youth, when thou wast refused, saith thy God. *For a small moment have I forsaken thee*; but with great mercies will I gather thee."

The above describes the suffering Israel endured, and will continue to endure because of their disobedience. He says that for a small moment I must forsake you, but then He would gather them at the end. Only when they have acknowledged that He is their God. Even though people might want to say that God has cast out Israel, He said Himself, "I will forsake them for a short while, but I will gather them again."

<u>Verse 10</u> **"For the mountains shall depart, and the hills be removed; but my kindness shall not depart from thee, neither shall the covenant of my peace be removed, saith the Lord that hath mercy on thee."** We must know who this Jesus was, and one thing for sure, He was not a Christian. The word Christian does not mean followers of Christ. This is another Christian lie. All the followers of Christ in the bible were Israelites, because Jesus the Christ Himself was one.

When the Gentiles shall come they would have to follow the ways of the Israelite. The Israelites have the key to the gates. If you try to enter in another way you are a thief.

<u>Luke 2:32</u> *"A light to lighten the Gentiles, and the glory of thy people Israel."* The separation is clear. The light of the Israelite would show the way to the entire world, even the Gentiles.

<u>Verse 34</u> "And Simeon blessed them, and said unto Mary his mother, Behold, this child is set for the fall and rising again of many in Israel; and for a sign which shall be spoken against;"

Both Christians and Muslims alike are teaching the lie that God had changed His mind. The Muslims are saying that Ishmael is now the chosen of God. In other words they are saying that the Bible and the Koran are both wrong, because both books confirm that Israel was, is, and will always be the first born, and family of God.

The Christians, not to be outdone, cannot see their role anywhere in the scriptures, are claiming now to be spirits **(spiritual Jews)**. While at the same time running after an Israelite (Paul) calling him a Christian, so that they can justify their actions he knows nothing of. Paul himself when talking about his brethren, refers to them as flesh and bones.

109

<u>**Romans 9:3-7**</u> **"For I could wish that myself were accursed from Christ for my brethren, my kinsmen according to the flesh; Who are Israelites: to whom pertaineth the adoption, and the glory, and the covenants, and the giving of the law, and the service of God, and the promises; Whose are the fathers, and of whom as concerning the flesh; Christ came who is over all, God blessed forever Amen."**

Paul identifies himself with his brethren who are Israelites in the flesh and not spirits, neither are they Christians. To understand fully, you must read further, Paul is grieving for his brethren who are refusing to follow the doctrine of Israel, so in **Verse 6** he says that all are not Israel which are in Israel. (Not all that were in the land Israel are of the seed of Israel or chosen). Then he goes on to confirm again in **Verse 7** that in Isaac shall the seed be called. **Again no spirit, and no Christian.**

This lesson is a two-fold one. It shows the relationship with God, the Israelites, and the Gentiles. It also shows that we have to be strong spiritually, if we have to achieve anything. What we have noticed also, is the fact that we are not all alike, we are not all equal, we are not all children of God. Some of us are born with grace, and some of us are not. Some of us will have to be saved by grace, some of us would not. Some of us are of the law, and some of us are not.

The other part of this story, is not only what the Christian teaches, that all are under grace, but they say that you must also have faith in the Christian god and their practices. Again not understanding anything about these matters. Christians make it their duty to also talk a lot about faith, but do they really know?

Faith in general does not only mean the doctrine and teachings of the children of Israel. There are those who have faith in Baal, there are those who have faith in strange philosophies, there are those who have faith in Lucifer, but the faith written about in the holy bible speaks only of the experiences of the children of Israel and their faith in their God, the God of Abraham, the God of Isaac and the God of Jacob. You will find the entire source for classification of this subject in **Hebrews 11 & Acts 7.**

FAITH & LAW

The chapter on grace should give us a clearer understanding of this very tossed-around-phrase. ***What does grace through faith mean?*** The last chapter ended in pointing out that the faith written about in the holy bible, has its root in the children of Israel. It is such a pity, that the children of slavery are refusing to accept their responsibility, and to carry out the duties set down by their God. Who were these people that were under the law?

The facts are clear, and the scriptures are plain. This bible speaks only of the people who are under the law, their story, their mistakes, their glory, their disappointments, their promise, their covenant, their doctrine and their practice. The bible speaks of their God, the God of Abraham, the God of Isaac, and the God of Jacob.

Some are ready to declare and quote the scriptures saying that a new covenant has been written. Indeed a new covenant has been written, but alas it has been written for the children of Israel again. Let us read from the same books that others read to confuse the minds of the ignorant. **Hebrews 8:8** "For finding fault with them, he saith, Behold, the days come, saith the Lord, when I will make a **new covenant with the house of Israel** and with the house of Judah." This same scripture can be found in **Jeremiah 31:34**. This is the confirmation that any covenant that was made, or will be made, will be with the children of Israel again.

Now that we have established this fact, let us go on to prove how all this is going to work for those who are not Israelites by birth or lineage, or not practising the teachings of the Israelites written about in the bible. It is said that in the last days there will be a lot of false prophets, and false teachings. Today more than ever there are so many calling themselves Israelites, that one must wonder. There are even white supremist groups that are calling themselves Israelites. I often wonder which bible they read? They probably printed their own, which would not be a bad idea for people who refuse to, or cannot face the truth.

The bible is very clear in its explanation concerning the days of the prophets and apostles. The bible does prove that God was never a Father to the whole world, but that the world may be saved through His children, the Israelites. Everyone outside the family of God that needed a favour from Him, had always turned to an Israelite, and not directly to God, starting from the book of Joshua. This is a story where it was written that Joshua had sent men to spy in the land of Jericho, and as the story unfolds, the men were protected and hidden by a harlot of that land. In granting the men of Israel the means to survive, and escape her own countrymen, she then asked that they too grant her a favour. That favour was, that they talk to their God for her, the God of Israel. I am very sorry to say, but the Christians are wrong. This bible is a discriminatory book. It is not of universal love. The scriptures will prove that she did not turn to God the way the Christians want you to believe. She asked the Israelites to help her, to talk to their God for her.

Joshua 2:9-11 shows that she is not claiming this God to be her own. "And she said unto the men, I know that the Lord hath given you the land, and that your terror is fallen upon us, and that all the inhabitants of the land faint because of you. For we have heard how the Lord dried up the water of the Red sea for you, when ye came out of Egypt; and what ye did unto the two kings of the Amorites, that were on the other side Jordan, Sihon and Og, whom ye utterly destroyed. And as soon as we had heard these things, our hearts did melt, neither did there remain any more courage in any man, because of you: *for the Lord your God*, he is God in heaven above, and in earth beneath."

In **Verses 12&13** her faith was in the works of the children of Israel, for she knew that the children of Israel were the children of God. "Now therefore, I pray you, swear unto me by the Lord, since I have shewed you kindness, that ye will also shew kindness unto my father's house, and give me a true token: And that ye will save alive my father, and my mother, and my brethren, and my sisters, and all that they have, and deliver our lives from death."

This harlot had discovered that the real God was against her people, therefore to whom and where could she turn? To the Israelites. In today's situation some philosophies would tell the Gentile (Christian) that they can go straight to God, which never happened in real biblical history. Christians teach that the death of Jesus changed all that. In this chapter we shall find out. In **Deuteronomy 7:6-7** "For thou art an holy people unto the Lord thy God: the Lord thy God hath chosen thee to be a special people unto himself, above all people that are upon the face of the earth. The Lord did not set his love upon you, nor choose you, because ye were more in number than any people, for ye were the fewest of all people:"

This last scripture is the base and foundation of faith. In **Verse 14**, the statement is very clear, it says "Thou shalt be blessed above all people:.." Is this the same God the Christians are talking about? Is this the God that loves everybody? No!

In the eighth chapter it is stated that God gave the commandments to the children of Israel. Now it is owned and controlled by Christianity so much so that people are calling the bible a Christian book. **Deuteronomy 8:1** "All the commandments which I command thee this day shall ye observe to do, that ye may live..." (God speaking to Israelites not Christians)

We should now turn to the books of Paul where all the confusion arises from, because of indebt misunderstanding. **Galatians 3:1-2** "O foolish Galatians, who hath bewitched you, that ye should not obey the truth, before whose eyes Jesus Christ hath been evidently set forth, crucified among you? This only would I learn of you, Received ye the Spirit by the works of the law, or by the hearing of faith?"

The Israelites get the Spirit through the work of the law, by keeping the Passover, the Day of Atonement, the Feast of the Tabernacle, the omission of wine drinking at the place of worship, by circumcision, by all the customs and the laws given by God to the prophets for their spiritual benefits. Then it also says in **Verse 2** "...or by the hearing of faith?" Now we are really defining faith. This faith is an offspring of the law. **Verse 3** "Are ye so foolish? having begun in the Spirit, are ye now made perfect by the flesh? If you are spiritual, you are spiritual. It is through that Spirit that you would achieve. To turn to the flesh would be a step down, and this is what the children of Israel are doing today by following the tradition of man-made philosophies. If you are spiritual, the flesh is not supreme to you. In some, the flesh is supreme over the Spirit. This should not be with the children of Israel.

Verse 4-5 "Have ye suffered so many things in vain? if it be yet in vain. He therefore that ministereth to you the Spirit, and worketh miracles among you, doeth he it by the works of the law, or by the hearing of faith?" The answer should be an easy one. One cannot attain spiritual power without the knowledge of the law.

Verse 6-8 "Even as Abraham believed God, and it was accounted to him for righteousness. Know ye therefore that they which are of faith, the same are the children of Abraham. And the scripture, foreseeing that *God would justify the heathen through faith*, preached before the gospel unto Abraham, saying, **In thee shall all nations be blessed**." In **Verse 8** it states "And the scripture..." Which scriptures did these people in the new testament read and study? THE OLD TESTAMENT. So there goes the Christian lie that the law in the old testament is past.

If you understand what the children of Abraham had to do, and you understand that they are the chosen of God, and you believe in what they did, and you follow the pattern of how they did it, then you can receive of God. **Verse 9-10** "So then they which be of faith are blessed with faithful Abraham. For as many as are of the works of the law are under the curse: for it is written, Cursed is every one that continueth not in all things which are written in the book of the law to do them." This verse is acknowledging that there are some of us who are indeed under the law. Those of us who are under the law, must live by the law, or we will die by the law. May I remind you that this is the new testament and there is such a thing as the law.

Verse 11 "But that no man is justified by the law in the sight of God, it is evident: for, The just shall live by faith." If a man does the law in a mechanical way, he is not justified. We should not be like the Pharisees, who made a great show of the law, without a purpose, and without God.

<u>**Verse 12**</u> "And the law is not of faith: but, **The man that doeth them shall live in them.**" The Israelites today, should have been taking this statement very serious.

<u>**Verse 13**</u> "Christ hath redeemed us from the curse of the law, being made a curse for us: for it is written, Cursed is every one that hangeth on a tree:" Christ has redeemed us from the **curse** of the law, not from the law. There is no statement that says in this bible, that the children of Israel no longer must keep the law. It is another Christian lie.

<u>**Verse 14**</u> "That the blessing of Abraham might come on the Gentiles through Jesus Christ; that we might receive the promise of the Spirit through faith."

What we must see among all these scriptures is that "God" means the God of Israel, whether you are under faith, grace or law. If you are going to come to God it has to be through the God of Abraham, Isaac and Jacob. If you are an Israelite you must keep the law. Others who are not would have to follow you, then they too shall be saved. Grace and faith comes through one channel and that is, in the law. Some would have to keep the law. Some would have to believe in the law that others are doing and some would have to turn to those doing the law to be saved.

What does it say in the last days? And they shall hold on to the skirt of those who are Jews, and say we will come with you, because we have heard that God is with you. This is the symbol, whether it is through grace or faith, you have to come through the narrow and straight path, through the God of Israel. <u>**Zechariah 8:23**</u> "Thus saith the Lord of hosts; In those days it shall come to pass, that ten men shall take hold out of all languages of the nations, even shall take hold of the skirt of him that is a Jew, saying, We will go with you: for we have heard that **God is with you.**"

These scriptures are not confusing, but confirming the fact that there is only one path. Some can go direct, others would have to follow the chosen of the most High, the children of Israel.

<u>**Galations 3:15-16**</u> "Brethren, I speak after the manner of men; Though it be but a man's covenant, yet if it be confirmed, no man disannulleth, or addeth thereto. Now to Abraham and his seed were the promises made.

115

He saith not, And to seeds, as of many; but as of one, And to thy seed, which is Christ.

Verse 17 "And this I say, that the covenant, that was confirmed before of God in Christ, *the law, which was four hundred and thirty years after, cannot disannul, that it should make the promise of none effect..*" "...cannot disannul..." means the law did not end with Jesus. It cannot be disannulled. The law cannot change.

Verse 18-20 "For if the inheritance be of the law, it is no more of promise: but God gave it to Abraham by promise. Wherefore then serveth the law? It was added because of transgressions, till the seed should come to whom the promise was made; and it was ordained by angels in the hand of a mediator. Now a mediator is not a mediator of one, but God is one." The law is sealed. **Verse 21** "Is the law then against the promises of God? God forbid: for if there had been a law given which could have given life, verily righteousness should have been by the law." **Verse 22-29** "But the scripture hath concluded all under sin, that the promise by faith of Jesus Christ might be given to them that believe. But before faith came, we were kept under the law, shut up unto the faith which should afterwards be revealed. Wherefore the law was our schoolmaster to bring us unto Christ, that we might be justified by faith. But after that faith is come, we are no longer under a school master. For ye are all the children of God by faith in Christ Jesus. For as many of you as have been baptized into Christ have put on Christ. There is neither Jew nor Greek, there is neither bond nor free, there is neither male nor female: for ye are all one in Christ Jesus. *And if ye be Christ's, then are ye Abraham's seed, and heirs according to the promise.*"

Before Christ came, the law was the school master for the children of Israel. Then Christ came in the flesh of Jesus, to teach that all might now be saved through the doctrine of Israel, through Christ. Do not confuse this with Christianity.

Now you know it is not a black thing, even though we have proven time and time again who are the real Israelites. If a person being polkadot follow the instructions of an Israelite teacher, worshipping the way of an Israelite, and not by themselves, then according to the scriptures, that person would be as one of Abraham's seed. The children of Israel were established even before their physical appearance, through their great-grandfather Abraham, then through his offspring in the book of Genesis.

It would only be fair to examine the end of the book, and its relation to the children of Israel, just so that Christian teachers, who shout every Sunday that there is no more law, and that we are all under grace can shut up once and for all. Bear in mind that God will seal one hundred and forty four thousand Israelites. Twelve thousand from each tribe. No Christians, nor Muslims allowed. **(Revelation 7)**
Revelation 22:1-6 "And he shewed me a pure river of water of life, clear as crystal, proceeding out of the throne of God and of the Lamb. In the midst of the street of it, and on either side of the river, *was there the tree of life, which bare twelve manner of fruits, and yielded her fruit every month: and the leaves of the tree were for the healing of the nations*. And there shall be no more curse: but the throne of God and of the Lamb shall be in it; and his servants shall serve him: And they shall see his face; and his name shall be in their foreheads. And there shall be no night there; and they need no candle, neither light of the sun; for the Lord God giveth them light: and they shall reign for ever and ever. And he said unto me, These sayings are faithful and true: and *the Lord God of the holy prophets* sent his angel to shew unto his servants the things which must shortly be done."

Yes, the book is confirming that there is no other way to salvation, but through the gates of Israel. The tree of life symbolizes the doctrine of the holy scriptures. The twelve manner of fruits symbolizes the twelve tribes of the House of Israel. Meaning, that the doctrine of the Israelites will save the nations upon this earth.

Verse 14-16 "Blessed are they that do his commandments, that they may have right to the tree of life, and may enter in through the gates into the city. For *without are dogs,* and sorcerers, and whoremongers, and murderers, and idolaters, and whosoever loveth and maketh a lie."

"Dogs" here mean strangers and Gentiles, teachers of false gods and strange philosophies. Let us examine Christianity in that context. First, this philosophy was started by Romans who were known to be Gentiles, and therefore not of God. What did Jesus call the Greek woman who was a Gentile? In **Mark 7:25-28** "For a certain woman, whose young daughter had an unclean spirit, heard of him, and came and fell at his feet: The woman was a Greek, a Syrophenician by nation; and she besought him that he would cast forth the devil out of her daughter. But Jesus said unto her, Let the children first be filled: for it is not meet to take the children's bread, and to cast it unto the **dogs.** And she answered and said unto him, Yes, Lord: yet the **dogs** under the table eat of the children's crumbs." The meaning is simple. The Israelites must have all blessings first, because they are the representatives of God on this earth. They alone are His children. The remainder can be given to whosoever needs it bad enough. (Jews first, then the Greek or anyone else).

This is repeated again in **Matthew 15:22-27**. "And, behold, a woman of Canaan came out of the same coasts, and cried unto him, saying, Have mercy on me, O Lord, thou Son of David; my daughter is grievously vexed with a devil. But he answered her not a word. And his disciples came and besought him, saying, Send her away; for she crieth after us. But he answered and said, **I am not sent but unto the lost sheep of the house of Israel.** Then came she and worshipped him, saying, Lord help me. But he answered and said, **It is not meet to take the children's bread, and to cast it to dogs.** And she said, Truth, Lord: yet the dogs eat of the crumbs which fall from their masters' table."

We must never forget the books of Paul. What did he say, and how did he identify himself? **Philippians 3:1-6** "Finally, my brethren, rejoice in the Lord. To write the same things to you, to me indeed is not grievous, but for you it is safe. **Beware of dogs**, beware of evil workers, beware of the concision. For **we are the circumcision, which worship God in the spirit, and rejoice in Christ Jesus, and have no confidence in the flesh. Though I might also have confidence in the flesh. If any other man thinketh that he hath whereof he might** trust in the flesh, I more: **Circumcised the eighth day, of the stock of Israel, of the tribe of Benjamin, an Hebrew of the Hebrews; as touching the law, a Pharisee**; Concerning zeal, persecuting the church; touching the righteousness which is in the law, blameless."

Now that we know who are called dogs, why should we want to follow after them and their strange philosophy. Even God discriminates against them. The skin colour should be of less importance than the philosophy. It is the philosophy of the Gentile that is poisonous to the spiritual life of an Israelite today, not the Gentiles themselves. Remember Titus, **Galatians 2:3**, Timotheus, **Acts 16:1**, Cornelius, **Acts 10:1**, and many more who came to the Israelites. It was wrong for the Israelites to go to them. The bible speaks clearly against it.

This is what the bible states that Israelites should do for anyone who needs to know the truth. **<u>Matthew 28:19-20</u>** "Go ye therefore, and **teach all nations**, baptizing them in the name of the Father, and of the Son, and of the Holy Ghost: **Teaching them to observe all things whatsoever I have commanded you**: and lo, I am with you alway, even unto the end of the world. Amen."

Jesus told His disciples to teach all nations, meaning Gentiles too, but teach them the things He commanded. He never sent them to be taught by the Christians (Gentiles). Gentiles can only teach what they know - the lie. The only things the disciples knew were the ways of an Israelite, and that only could they have taught to those who would need to know, and accept the word of truth.

Matthew 7:6-8. **<u>Verse 6</u>** "Give not that which is holy unto the dogs, neither cast ye your pearls before swine, lest they trample them under their feet, and turn again and rend you."

The children of the circumcision are a holy people. They are like precious jewels to the God of Abraham, Isaac and Jacob. If they only know who they are, and return to the flock, under one Shepherd, our God. After all, salvation is of the Jews. Why search for it among dogs?

I AM DIFFERENT

There are some things in life I'm trying to understand
I was looking for answers as hard as I can
I listened to Christians every Sunday
I listened attentively to what they would say
They talk so much about universal love
That all the world should
Love and love and love
There is a God up there they say
Who loves all mankind in the same old way

I'm in the middle now - my eyes can see
I looked all around but no love for me
The man with the cross he burns it with hate
The man in the cloth - Oh, he's a mistake
Took all my money and said to have faith
He said I need to be poor so the world could see
I need to be doped without a family
So that he would collect a lot of money
To tell the world he did it for me

Now he's so rich and I'm still poor
What a fool I've been - dumb to the core
The jail that I know is the only home I've got
With three meals a day and a roof at the top
Whenever I'm out it starts over again
My life is re-cycled with poverty and pain

The things they told me are hard to believe
Now that I know so stupid it seems
All men are created equal
This is what they say
How can this be - when they are blind and I can see
They talk of this God they wish they had
Making themselves look good and me so bad

I am different - I know there is something in me
That they never tell - cause of inferiority
How come my blood has sickle cell
And there is woolly hair upon my head
Am I equal to others? I think I'm not
I am superior in strength and in spirit there's a lot
How come there's fibroid in my woman's womb?
Like Sarah, Rebekah and Rachel too

They never told me of the liniment under my skin
To protect it from cancer and those terrible things
Of all the world God chose me
If you don't believe read Amos Three
So please Mr. Christian
With all your power and well to do
Can't you see that I'm different from you?
I'm of God and you're of Baal
Wherever you came from and wherever you went
The bible says that I'm different.

IS GOD DIVINE?

To some people this can be a very offensive question, but let us examine it very carefully, since it is being used by teachers of ignorance. Is God really divine?

The answer is no. This myth is shared by most philosophies including Christianity. These teachers want everyone to believe that they are serving the right God. Therefore making themselves holier than thou, using all sorts of words, having no knowledge of its origin or meaning. Their main aim is to impress their parishioners.

We are going to explore in the divine darkness for proof. But first allow me to point out a few facts about the evils of the philosophy that started the myth that the Almighty God, the Creator of all things; the true and living God; the God of Abraham, the God of Isaac and the God of Jacob; the God written about in the Holy Scriptures, is divine. If you want to know the truth, they are right. Their god is divine. The god of the Christian is a divine god.

Let's examine the meaning of the word from the English dictionary. (1) Pertaining to, proceeding from, or of the nature of God or of a god, sacred. (2) Addressed, or offered up to God. (3) Altogether excellent or admirable. (4) A theologian or clergyman. If you look very carefully you would notice that a god is being used here along with a theologian. Who is a theologian? Is this man written about in the bible? NO! The same goes for clergyman.

According to the bible, divine is earthly. It is more evil than good. It pertains to adopted spirits, wizards, witches, witchcraft and things of this nature. No person collecting money for services rendered through the help of earth-bound spirits can be of God. The person who does these things cannot and does not call upon the God written of, or about in the bible. They call on the spirits of the air and the spirits of the earth that are called familiar spirits, or spirits of **divination**, who themselves believe that they are gods. A person that makes his or her money consulting through these spirits are witches and wizards, who deal in witchcraft.

God's people have the ability to also do spiritual things. They do them with the knowledge of God.

There is however, a strong condemnation of witchcraft in the bible, a warning to the children of God. __Deuteronomy 18:10-13__ "There shall not be found among you any one that maketh his son or his daughter to pass through the fire, or that useth **divination**, or an observer of times, or an enchanter, or a witch. Or a charmer, or a **consulter** with familiar spirits, or a wizard, or a necromancer. For all that do these things are an abomination unto the Lord: and because of these abominations the Lord thy God doth drive them out from before thee. Thou shalt be perfect with the Lord thy God."

You must be aware that Christianity is a philosophy that worships the dead. Let's examine their customs. How they handle their dead, and how they baptize are two of the issues we will be dealing with in this chapter.

THE CHRISTIAN DEAD

Worshipping of the dead might seem to some a strange concept. You are probably asking yourselves, how can one worship the dead. Well, let us start with a very simple but extremely accurate definition of this pagan practice. Worshipping of the dead can be defined as one engaging in the act of worship who does not call upon the God mentioned in the holy bible, the God of Abraham, Isaac and Jacob, but nevertheless calls upon a god, or another spiritual force. Any spiritual force other than the Almighty God referred to in the holy bible, would be adopted spirits or entities. Here is an example, if you worship continually at a particular place, and in a particular way, the unseen is bound to place itself before you. If you do not do the things of God, then you are most certainly worshipping Lucifer. As simple as that. These adopted spirits like to be called gods, and to receive praises. In simple terms, you are calling on earth-bound spirits, spirits of men and women who have lived before and are now dead.

The professional practitioners of this evil habit, do not follow the instructions given by God to His people.

The God of the Israelites is the God of the living. Any other god would have to be a false god, and as I mentioned before, familiar spirits and spirits of divination like to be called gods. They are actually the gods (spirits) of the dead. There is even more revealing evidence of the outright worshipping of the dead that some practice through ignorance, while others, through deliberate acts.

Let's see what Paul said to the Athenians at Mars Hill who worshipped the dead. **Acts 17:23** states "For as I passed by, and beheld your devotions, I found an altar with this inscription, TO THE UNKNOWN GOD. Whom therefore ye ignorantly worship, him declare I unto you."

God Himself states in **Matthew 22:32** "I am the God of Abraham, and the God of Isaac, and the God of Jacob? God is not the God of the dead, but of the living." There should be no doubt in our minds that the dead are unclean and should play no part in the sanctuary of God, or in our personal relationship with our God.

The dead have no place among the living. **Ecclesiastes 9:5** says "For the living know that they shall die: but the dead know not any thing, neither have they any more a reward; for the memory of them is forgotten." This has a two folded meaning because those that worship the dead lack understanding and shall remain in the congregation of the dead. These are the living dead. Read **Proverbs 21:16**. "The man that wandereth out of the way of understanding shall remain in the congregation of the dead."

Matthew 23:27 "Woe unto you, scribes and Pharisees, hypocrites! for ye are like unto whitened sepulchres, which indeed appear beautiful outward, but are within full of dead men's bones, and of all **uncleanness**." Think about it for awhile, is Jesus really saying that the dead are unclean? Yes He is! Then why does the Christian church embrace the dead?

That brings us to a another aspect of Christianity and their custom of burial. We should always remember that it was the Christians who designed the cemetery as we know it today. We are so strong on following, that we are prepared to follow the practice of Christianity to the last breath without doubting.

Worshipping of the dead openly started with the heathens in Babylon, Egypt, Ethiopia, Canaan and eventually the Gentiles (Greek and Romans). It was the Roman Catholic church, the mother of the Christian organization that is responsible for the cover-up today, because again they too read the bible.

At the time that Rome ruled the world they were pagans. They had gods for everything, every event and special occasion. The Christian church openly disobeyed the statutes of God, replacing them with paganism.

God says in the books of Moses which time of the year is His New Year, yet in the sixteenth century King Charles of France, a Christian, replaced it with the symbol of the pagan gods. **Exodus 12:2** "This month shall be unto you the beginning of months: it shall be the first month of the year to you." He went on to name the month, which would be in the spring, when the earth is alive. The beginning of life. The first of the Zodiac. **Exodus 13:4** "This day came ye out in the month Abib." This time usually falls in the months of March - April.

What had they replaced God's beginning with? January, named after the Roman god Janus. Who it was said, had two faces, one looking towards the south, while the other looking towards the north. This image was a familiar sight at the doorway of the houses of the Roman elite and places of pagan worship. The next was February. The word February comes from the Latin word "februa." At this time the pagans kept their feast. It was called the feast of purification to their gods. It was this same event the early Christians turned into what they then called candlemas which was a total mockery to the Almighty God. Juno Regina was the goddess of womanhood and marriage. Ops was the goddess of wealth. Mercury was the god of orators and quite an orator in Roman fables. This explains why the people of Lystra thought Paul (an Israelite) to be the god Mercury.

Acts 14:11-12 "And when the people saw what Paul had done, they lifted up their voices, saying in the speech of Lycaonia, The gods are come down to us in the likeness of men. And they called Barnabas, Jupiter; and Paul, Mercurius, because he was the chief speaker."

These gods were associated with various events in life. They were then merged into the church of Rome and all these gods and goddesses were renamed and called saints to please and impress the parishioners. Today there is a saint that one can pray to for help for every affliction, occupation and disease in the Catholic church. The children of slaves are in a deplorable state because they refuse to let go of the skirt of the child and mother of this pagan philosophy known as Christianity, and turn away ungodliness from Jacob.

Did you ever read any scripture or scriptures in the bible telling you to have **respect for the dead**? Well I have not seen any, yet christian teachers would tell us and we would believe. The bible says that after death comes judgment. The bible also says that death is the enemy of God.

<u>**I Corinthians 15:26**</u> "The last **enemy** that shall be destroyed is **death.**" If the bible is saying that death is the enemy of God, **then what is the dead body doing at your church's altar? Why do Christians take their dead to their altar and keep a service over that dead body? Do you think that Christians, or any other philosophy that practices this evil can answer this question?** I think not, unless they lie again, as always.

Why are most Christian churches built in the midst of the burial place of the dead? This is indeed a sad situation, but no one is taking it serious. In <u>**Psalms 115:17**</u> "The dead praise not the Lord, neither any that go down into silence." We learn that the dead cannot praise God, and if I might add, those that mix with them, their eyes cannot see this evil.

Let's look at flowers and the Christian dead. Did anyone ever stop to think that this practice could also be wrong? Well it is wrong, and it is out of the way. It is not of God. It was never given to the children of Israel as a statute, nor a law, nor a commandment. Again it is to be made very clear, that the praising of the dead and the general use of flowers at the graveside is witchcraft, practiced by pagans especially in Europe.

FLOWERS

To define this evil practice, we must first of all find the purpose. Here is a typical example for the use of flowers on the dead, or at the home of the dead, or in the church, where the deceased Christian attended, and finally at the graveside along with the cross. Pretend that you are a bee-keeper and you need to attract bees from one area to another. First you would have to transfer some of the honey from the old area to the new location. After you have done this, the bees would then follow the smell, or whatever attracts them to honey, right to the new location. It is somewhat similar in the spiritual world.

First, you would identify the flowers with the dead. Even without the physical presence of the flowers you still would be able to smell them, and you would know that the spirit of the dead is visiting, especially the jasmine flower. The next stage without going into much detail, is to decorate your altar with the same flowers. Christian Priests do this so they can make the same adopted spirit feel comfortable and at home among the living. The cross also plays a similar role, from the grave to the altar, and from the altar to the grave. It really does not make much difference, it is just downright evil. If this was such a holy practice why did they not bury Jesus and put a cross at His grave? After all this is the same man they claim to be following. Instead it was the cross that killed Him.

No person written about in the bible had anything to do with flowers, or the cross at the time of the dead, or used it as a symbol of worship. **There was never any service at a burial place, no service in the church for the dead, or any such evil and unclean practice. There is no proof in the bible of any of these Christian actions. This practice is pagan to the core.**

The custom of putting things on the grave started in the reign of Josiah, who ruled Jerusalem from the tender age of eight for thirty one years. Proof is found in **II Chronicles 34:1-4** and this is what is stated in <u>**Verse 4**</u>. "And they brake down the altars of Baalim in his presence; and the images, that were on high above them, he cut down; and the groves, and the carved images, and the molten images, he brake in pieces, and made dust of them, and strowed it upon the graves of them that had sacrificed unto them." The lesson here, is that they worshipped with the symbols and images of false gods, and these same images were placed on their graves. This is exactly the same way the symbol of the cross and flowers are placed on the graves of Christians.

The scriptures where you will find the use of flowers are never live flowers, but artistically drawn in various designs by the children of Israel. It was never used for, or among the dead. **Exodus 25:31-33** "And thou shalt make a candlestick of pure gold: of beaten work shall the candlestick be made: his shaft, and his branches, his bowls, his knops, and his flowers, shall be of the same. And six branches shall come out of the sides of it; three branches of the candlestick out of the one side, and three branches of the candlestick out of the other side: Three bowls made like unto almonds, with a knop and a flower in one branch; and three bowls made like almonds in the other branch, with a knop and a flower: so in the six branches that come out of the candlestick." **Exodus 37:17** "And he made the candlestick of pure gold: of beaten work made he the candlestick; his shaft, and his branch, his bowls, his knops, and his flowers, were of the same:" **Numbers 8:4** "And this work of the candlestick was of beaten gold, unto the shaft thereof, unto the flowers thereof, was beaten work: according unto the pattern which the Lord had shewed Moses, so he made the candlestick."

All these scriptures are dealing with instructions from the Almighty God Himself to His servant. Even in the days of Solomon the same was done.

I Kings 6:18 "And the cedar of the house within was carved with knops and open flowers: all was cedar; there was no stone seen." Also **II Chronicles 4:21** "And the flowers, and the lamps, and the tongs, made he of gold, and that perfect gold;" This is even more proof that the flowers written about in the scriptures are indeed works of art and not live flowers that were used for works done by witches and wizards.

Take a look at the way Christians baptize, leading you to believe that you are born again. To be "born again" is in the bible, but do the Christian teachers adhere to the instructions written about in the bible? No! So then, how can one be born again in Christianity?

BAPTISM

This is the Christian's favourite scripture to justify their action of backward baptism.

Colossians 2:12-13 "Buried with him in baptism, wherein also ye are risen with him through the faith of the operation of God, who hath raised him from the dead. And you, being dead in your sins and the uncircumcision of your flesh, hath he quickened together with him, having forgiven you all trespasses;" Paul is speaking to Gentiles, (uncircumcision means non-Israelites). It is so typical of this philosophy to see everything in a physical way, that even the word buried to them would mean lying on your back so you may raise in Christ. Now let's all sit back and have a nice laugh, ha! ha! That brings to mind how the devil sees the things of God. The evil man can never fully understand holy things.

Baptism can be defined as submission, a new beginning, a crossing over from the physical to the spiritual. To be baptized, or to allow a man that is a representative of this strange philosophy to push you backwards, telling you that you are now born again is wrong, Wrong! Wrong! Can anything backward move forward with a degree of speed, accuracy and perfection?

The bible states in **Luke 14:26** that you must hate your mother, your father, your brethren, then pick up your cross and follow me. These are the words of Jesus. Is this what it means? Is the bible saying to hate everyone? The answer is no. Note that Jesus was alive and well, not yet killed on the cross when he made this statement. Can fools understand the works of the wise? No again. The bible is not a Christian book therefore do not expect Christians to understand the writing of the prophets, saints and apostles.

It is not given to the Gentiles yet to understand the book of the prophets. Until the doctrine of Israel has been taught all over the world the end will never come. The enemies of God are the ones who go backwards. This is the blessings of Dan. **Genesis 49:16-17** "Dan shall judge his people, as one of the tribes of Israel. Dan shall be a serpent by the way, an adder in the path, that biteth the horse heels, so that his rider shall **fall backward**." Note that Dan's enemy would fall backwards and Dan was a chosen of God, an Israelite.

Let us also read the story of the Ark of God in **I Samuel 4:18** "And it came to pass, when he made mention of the ark of God, that he fell from the seat backward by the side of the gate, and his neck brake, and he died:.."

The above verse is the sign of disaster. To be falling backward is a sign of spiritual stagnation and death. This is a very distasteful sign. Even though logic is the hardest to believe in, it is the only substance we have. The bible says that the acceptable way to pray is to humble yourself before your Creator on your face, or on your knees with your hands and eyes towards heaven. Imagine now you are before your altar. Would you turn your back on your altar? No, that would be wrong. Would you face your altar, on your knees, with your back on the ground, the way the singer Madonna did in her video, "Like a prayer"? No! But this is the way the pagans used to pray, putting all emphasis on their backs, allowing their sexual organs to be before their altars.

Especially women, who were being used in those days as tools by these perverts for the satisfaction of their pagan lust.

To pray backwards is to expose your spiritual nakedness, and if baptism also means submission, why then should you be baptized on your back? **Lamentation 1:8-9** "Jerusalem hath grievously sinned; therefore she is removed: all that honoured her despise her, because they have seen her nakedness: yea, she sigheth, and turneth backward. Her filthiness is in her skirts; she remembereth not her last end; therefore she came down wonderfully: she had no comforter. O Lord, behold my affliction: for the enemy hath magnified himself."

Israel is seen here through the eyes of God, as a woman and because of her following of false gods and strange philosophies she kept going backwards, and not forward in progress. In doing the things that were backwards, she was exposing herself, allowing strangers to see beneath her skirts, all of her nakedness and shame. **Jeremiah 32:33-34** "And they turned unto me the back, and not the face: though I taught them, rising up early and teaching them, yet they have not hearkened to receive instruction. But they set their abominations in the house, which is called by my name, to defile it."

Look what happened to other enemies of God. Jesus was in the garden with His disciples, when His enemies approached including Judas, but when the spirit came upon Him and He identified Himself, they fell backward. **John 18:6** "As soon then as he had said unto them, I am he, they went backward, and fell to the ground."

The first baptism was not done on the back, as a matter of fact, it could not have been done that way at all, because the children of Israel were moving forward very fast. The bible says that this baptism should be an example to follow, because this was the first baptism with Fire and the Holy Spirit and Water. **I Corinthians 10:1-6** "Moreover, brethren, I would not that ye should be ignorant, how that all our fathers were under the cloud, and all passed through the sea; **And were all baptized** unto Moses in the cloud and in the sea; And did all eat the same spiritual meat; And did all drink the same spiritual drink: for they drank of that spiritual Rock that followed them: and that Rock was Christ. But with many of them God was not well pleased: for they were overthrown in the wilderness. **Now these things were our examples,** to the intent we should not lust after evil things, as they also lusted." It is typical of Christians to quote the baptism in the new testament, and not understanding the first one done by God Himself to the children of Israel. God had baptized the children of Israel twice. First at the Red sea, then again at Jordan, and both times the children of Israel had to be moving forward. When ignorance is bliss it's folly to be wise.

The word of God is so clear yet believers are so few. Let us all give cheers to the Great Whore, for she must indeed be great. Just take a look at what is left of God's chosen people today, isn't this a sad situation, To watch them cry to Baal again, to watch them mourn over false gods and strange philosophies? It is indeed a shame. They keep serving a divine god that has ears but can't hear, eyes but can't see and they have become like unto them.

THE SPIRIT OF DIVINATION

To examine the use of this word "divine" used by Christians, we must start where it is first found to be attractive. **Hebrews 9:1** "Then verily the first covenant had also ordinances of divine service, **and a worldly sanctuary.**"

Reading this scripture you will even be tempted to believe what others are saying. This verse may seem like a confirmation, but it is not. Please note that the first sanctuary was made by hands, earthly. It was divine because it was spiritual but earthly and of a worldly flavour. **II Peter 1:3-4** "According as his divine power hath given unto **us** all things that pertain unto life and godliness, through the knowledge of him that hath called **us** to glory and virtue: Whereby are given unto **us** exceeding great and precious promises: that by these ye might be partakers of the divine nature, having escaped the corruption that is in the world through lust." He gave the Israelites (us) spiritual power over all spirits (godliness), to control them upon this earth

He gave the children of Israel life and godliness (saintly power). He himself called them gods in **Isaiah 41:23**. He fed them with angel's food in **Psalms 78:25**. In other words they were called gods, because of the spiritual power given to them by God himself.

We must see this bible in the context in which it is written. First, we must know who is speaking, and to whom. God has given to His people the power physically to do spiritual things. I think this needs to be explained a little more. If you strike a match, it is a physical action, but the purpose can be a spiritual one. You may light a candle, or burn incense, but the physical action has a spiritual reaction. This is the knowledge that God gave to the children of Israel, because the other side also had some knowledge given to them by Lucifer.

There is a myth circulating among the Christians that gives one the impression that Satan is a weakling and a wimp. Some Christian preachers on television are leading their audience to believe that they have the power to say "Satan get behind me." and he will. We must understand that their statement is a gross misconception and is not true at all. God Himself knows the power of Satan, because in creation Satan (Lucifer) was there and had the knowledge of what went on. Read (The Truth the Lie and the Bible, the chapter on The First Family). Satan stood face to face with God and made deals with Him. Can these lying practitioners do that? Take for instance the story of Job in **Job 1:6-7** "Now there was a day when the sons of God came to present themselves before the Lord, and Satan came also among them. And the Lord said unto Satan, Whence cometh thou? Then Satan answered the Lord, and said, From going to and fro in the earth, and from walking up and down in it."

Please read the entire chapter for more details. You will find a repeat of this in **Zechariah 3:1** "And he shewed me Joshua the high priest standing before the angel of the Lord, and Satan standing at his right hand to resist him."

The teachers of Christianity will tell you after you have proven them to be liars, that since Jesus died it all changed. As a matter of fact, for Christians the death of Jesus changed everything. This is their way out, through this overused excuse.

In **Matthew 4:10** "Then said Jesus unto him, Get thee hence, Satan." Here you see Satan taking control of Jesus's best friend and disciple Peter. If Satan was this weakling and wimp that the Christians are painting, why does God have to wait so long to bind him, then let him go and bind him again? Let us look at the power and authority of the father of evil. Jesus even mentioned to Peter that Satan wanted him, but He, (Jesus) would pray for him. **Luke 22:31-32**. Does this force sound like a wimp?

Luke 10 again shows that the seventy that Jesus sent forth with power were all Israelites, and they had power over devils which are servants of Satan and not Satan. It is said in **Verse 18** "And he said unto them, I beheld Satan as lightning fall from heaven."

We have read that death will be the last enemy of God and Lucifer is the controller of death. Yet we don't seem to understand what the scriptures are saying. **Revelation 2:24** "But unto you I say, and unto the rest in Thyatira, as many as have not this doctrine, and which have not known the *depths of Satan*, as they speak; I will put upon you none other burden." It was Jesus who said "Get thee hence, Satan." but these teachers are not Jesus, and they are not of Israel, so then who are they? How sound can their teachings be? Jesus in His day, did not even give all of Israel this power. He gave His twelve, who had to go out and teach it to other Israelites, about their power and their glory. Any other philosophy would be wrong.

This being or spirit called Satan stood in the presence of God Almighty. He even stood face to face and tempted Jesus. Now someone tell me, can a man without heavenly power control him? We must first find out if Satan stood before a person without the power of God. Without the knowledge, wisdom and understanding of this matter, whom do you think would control who? We may now return to our topic on divination.

God was protecting His own (Israelites) by giving them spiritual knowledge and power over things of the earth and nature. Divine really means to penetrate, to look into, to dwell into things unseen. Things that are worldly, yet spiritual. **Understanding that all spiritual things are not of God.**

Here is an example; **ISamuel 28:8**. "And Saul disguised himself, and put on other raiment, and he went, and two men with him, and they came to the woman by night: and he said, I pray thee, **divine unto me by the familiar spirit**, and bring me him up, whom I shall name unto thee."

Micah 3:6 "Therefore night shall be unto you, that ye shall not have a vision; and it shall be dark unto you, that ye **shall not divine**; and the sun shall go down over the prophets, and the day shall be dark over them."

These divine men and women were working contrary to God's law divining for money. Look around you today, everyone that does their divining and taking your money, are letting you believe that it is of God, but I am telling you now that it is not. Nothing here is saying that God is divine or that He is the spirit of divination, or is fulfilled with divinity. No!

Let us read for a fuller understanding about the spirit of divination. There is the story of Balak, a ruler of the Moabites who wanted evil on the children of Israel, so he sent for Balaam. You would know him today as a witch doctor, or an obeah man, a man with spiritual knowledge but not of God, to do the work of iniquity on the children of Israel. **Numbers 22:6-7** "Come now therefore, I pray thee, curse me this people; for they are too mighty for me: peradventure I shall prevail, that we may smite them, and that I may drive them out of the land: for I wot that he whom thou blessest is blessed, and he whom thou cursest is cursed. And the elders of Moab and the elders of Midian departed with the **rewards of divination in their hand**; and they came unto Balaam, and spake unto him the words of Balak." By reading the last scripture I hope you will understand the point I am trying to make, but the next scripture will confirm the previous scripture of **II Peter 1:3-4**.

In the following scripture God is saying that the spirit of divination and enchantments should not have any effect on the children of Israel. **Numbers 23:23 "Surely there is no enchantment against Jacob, neither is there any divination against Israel: according to this time it shall be said of Jacob and of Israel, What hath God wrought!"**

The battle line is drawn. The children were taught by God, therefore they should not be using any adopted spirits, nor spirits of divination. This is in the book of the laws. **Ezekiel 12:24** "For there shall be no more any vain vision nor flattering divination within the house of Israel."

II Kings 17:17 "And they caused their sons and their daughters to pass through the fire, and used divination and enchantments, and sold themselves to do evil in the sight of the Lord, to provoke him to anger."

Ezekiel 13:6-9 "They have seen vanity and lying divination, saying, The Lord saith: and the Lord hath not sent them: and they have made others to hope that they would confirm the word. Have ye not seen a vain vision, and have ye not spoken a

lying divination, whereas ye say, The Lord saith it; albeit I have not spoken? Therefore thus saith the Lord God; Because ye have spoken vanity, and seen lies, therefore, behold, I am against you, saith the Lord God. And mine hand shall be upon the prophets that see vanity, and that divine lies: they shall not be in the assembly of my people, neither shall they be written in the writing of the house of Israel, neither shall they enter into the land of Israel: and ye shall know that I am the Lord God."**

By this time the whole context of our spiritually was in the hands of liars. **Jeremiah 14:14** "Then the Lord said unto me, The prophets prophesy lies in my name: I sent them not, neither have I commanded them, neither spake unto them: they prophesy unto you a **false vision and divination, and a thing of nought,** and the deceit of their heart."

Now if the spirit of divination is so evil and against the laws of God, how then can the Almighty God be divine? This is another terrible lie that is responsible for our ills and our torment. We must examine the things that we do in the name of God and find out which god.

Today this practice in divinity is rampant, and the spirit of divination is on the rise because of hard times. A typical example is in the book of Paul. **Acts 16:16** "And it came to pass, as we went to prayer, a certain damsel **possessed with a spirit of divination** met us, which brought her masters much gain by soothsaying:" Please note who was getting the gain from this spirit of divination, and who was getting the pain. This is the most plain verse on this topic.

Since Christianity can be defined as a cult, and practitioners of witchcraft, it would be dangerous to be ignorant of it. Jim Jones in Jonestown to David Koresh in Waco Texas are the living example of its end. Some of these Christian groups apply their teachings for wealth, and do get away with it, and progress through their evil practice. Why? Because their god is evil, and together they are all in one accord. But for a black person, this wealth can never materialize through this mean, because the children of slaves are not the children of this evil. So naturally they would have to accept spiritual hand-outs and suffer at its mercy.

As a matter of fact, the countries that boast this evil are themselves the poorest in the world today. There is one thing however that I can say, and that is, evil is always easier to be done with the spirit of divination. There is a saying that man does not have to study to be bad. It is natural unto him and so are the spirits of divination.

The spirits of divination are really lost souls that have passed on before and are now in the state of torment, confusion, and misery. They are sometimes called adopted spirits, or entities. If life had provided us with a count from one to ten, and you were under the control of an adopted spirit that knew only up to three in its lifetime, your life automatically would stagnate at three. This is therefore the cause of the downfall of Israelites living today, because they entertain and recycle spirits that are not progressive because of their old ways. They never get to ten regardless of how hard they try. To conclude, let me say this, worshipping is the act of honouring, idolizing or reverencing an object, person or unseen being. Before there was one God known to the world everyone worshipped spirits, or multiple gods. Especially in the continent of Africa.

Are there any progress in these lands to make one proud? No! We should now ask ourselves who is the master of deception? Let us see what the scriptures have to say regarding this matter. **Revelation 12:9** says, "And the great dragon was cast out, that old serpent, called the Devil, and Satan, which deceiveth the whole world: he was cast out into the earth, and his angels were cast out with him."

The real meaning of divine is dealing with earth-bound spirits, or spiritual things done by physical hands. **It is not heavenly, and it is not holy.** After reading and studying with me, do you still think that the Almighty God, the God of Abraham, the God of Isaac and the God of Jacob is divine? What kind of a person is a doctor of divinity?

Would he or she be of God? No educational institution can give anyone this spiritual knowledge. This must come direct from the spirit of understanding. This knowledge must come from God. This understanding would only be given to an Israelite. **I write therefore with confidence, and no compromising.**

OUR NEW YEAR

Here comes the beginning of things
Here comes the spring
Here comes the blossoms
And the flowers they bring
Here comes Aries the astrological dream
The first of the Zodiacs
Just like Abib

Here's written the facts
With the things we should do
In Exodus Twelve and Verse Two
You'll find the month and a little bit more
In Thirteen and Verse Four
Tis the time when the earth is alive
Tis the time when the birds arrive
Here comes the truth we all must share
Here comes the beginning of our
NEW YEAR

This is the statute of our God
Given to the children of Israel
And His instructions we should hear
That the month of Abib
Is the first of the Year
Let's laugh and sing and forget our pain
Tis the time of rejoicing
A HAPPY NEW YEAR

STARTING OVER AGAIN

Let us start with our children, and teach them the right way, starting with colours. The colours of the Israelites, the colours of the children of slavery are Red, White, Purple and Blue.

You can order a flag professionally painted and mounted on canvas, in various sizes for your altar, or for your place of worship. It can be given as a gift to someone important to you, or even for decoration in your living room, or you may place it over your bed etc.

Contact

Israelite Nation World Wide Ministires
@

www.israelitenation.com

contact@israelitenation.com

COLOUR YOUR OWN ISRAELITE FLAG USING THE COLOURS APPROVED BY GOD HIMSELF

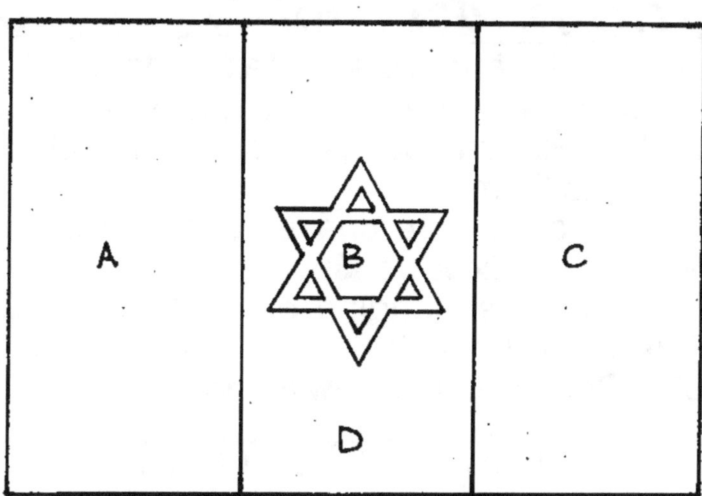

FIG.1

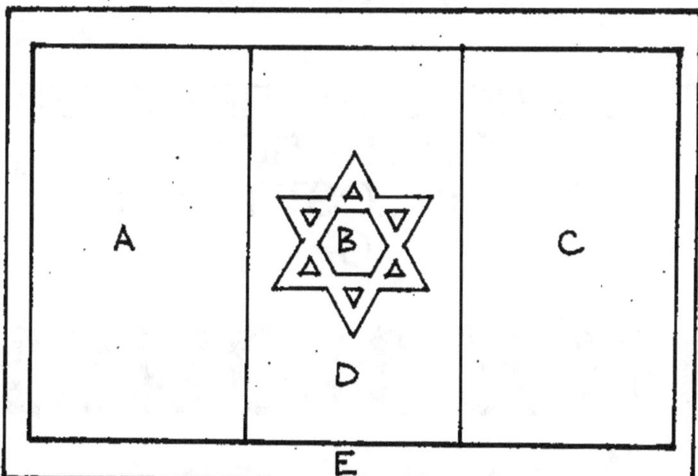

FIG.2

A:- PURPLE **B:-** Outline of star in RICH BLUE **C:-** RED (scarlet)
D:- WHITE **E:-** very LIGHT BLUE **FIG: 1** ORIGINAL DESIGN
For the **HOUSE OF ISRAEL** **FIG: 2** Artist impression
(Patrick Stoute) Additional border line of blue

COLOURS OF THE ISRAELITES

EXODUS 26:1 "Moreover thou shalt make the tabernacle with ten curtains of fine **Twined Linen, and Blue, and Purple, and Scarlet**: with cherubims of cunning work shalt thou make them."
These colours were chosen and approved by God Himself. **Exodus 39:43**
For fuller understanding of the flag And the colours used on the other page Read The Stolen Colours in the New Edition of

"THE TRUTH THE LIE AND THE BIBLE"

THESE COLOURS REPRESENT THE NATION OF THE LOST TRIBES OF

THE HOUSE OF ISRAEL